W9-CCX-620

Curriculum Renewal

Allan A. Glatthorn

Association for Supervision and Curriculum Development
125 N. West Street, Alexandria, Virginia 22314-2798

The Author

ALLAN A. GLATTHORN is Professor of Education, Graduate School of Education, University of Pennsylvania, where he teaches and conducts research in supervision, curriculum, and school leadership. He was for more than 25 years a school teacher, supervisor, and principal. His text on curriculum development, *Curriculum Leadership*, has just been published by Scott Foresman. Author of *Differentiated Supervision* (published by ASCD in 1984), he is currently consulting with school districts across the country in implementing a system of differentiated professional development and in curriculum renewal.

Copyright 1987 by the Association for Supervision and Curriculum Development.

All rights reserved. No part of this publication may be reproduced or transmitted in any form or by any means, electronic or mechanical, including photocopy, recording, or any information storage and retrieval system, without permission in writing from the publisher.

ASCD publications present a variety of viewpoints. The views expressed or implied in this publication are not necessarily official positions of the Association.

Price: $8.75
ASCD Stock Number: 611-86060
ISBN: 0-87120-143-7
Library of Congress
  Catalog Card Number: 86-72998

LB
2806.15
G58
1987

Curriculum Renewal

Foreword

ALLAN GLATTHORN IS A CAPABLE SCHOLAR, COMPETENT PRACTITIONER, and prolific author. Even for an individual with such varied qualifications, this book is a remarkable achievement.

To the casual reader, it is indeed the product as advertised. In a clear, concise, direct, and personal manner, Glatthorn makes good on his promise to take the mystery out of "doing" curriculum. His terminology is specifically defined and consistently applied. His documentation is realistic, tangible, and useful.

The book is fascinating in the ease with which the author draws upon research from effective schools, significant reports, ASCD publications, and such authorities as Boyer, Goodlad, and Sizer.

In the process Glatthorn shares his own significant insights about teachers—that they know better than they teach, their decisions about curriculum typically reflect compromises, and the way they think about a subject profoundly influences how they teach. He stresses views held widely—that teachers should be involved in assessments or evaluations—and others not so well accepted—that, in a sense, curriculum grows out of staff development.

Perhaps a single guideline is most profound: do not assume all educational goals to be curriculum goals.

But a more careful examination reveals that Glatthorn has provided an exemplary model of the curriculum as advocated. The book itself is a curriculum, including both the plans for learning and their actual delivery. The four types of curriculums depicted by Glatthorn are readily apparent. Mastery (structured, basic) curriculum is most prevalent in the descriptions of establishing goals in Chapter 2 and reviewing fields of study in Chapter 3. In these discussions Glatthorn prunes as well as cultivates to ensure clear purposes and uncluttered plans. The rationale for a consensus curriculum illustrates both his academic scholarship and his political savvy. Yet rigor and quality are never sacrificed to realism and practicality.

Organic (nonstructured, basic) curriculum is manifest in the balance between leader initiative and faculty involvement as well as between research evidence and teacher judgment. It is suggested that the leader persuade a department faculty to accept primary responsibility for a particular goal or contribute to fulfillment of subgoals; conversely, the leader is admonished to solicit faculty advice at each stage of curriculum development and to disseminate interpretations widely. It is recommended that summary reports of expert opinion be circulated and serve as the basis of teacher dialogs, which create an atmosphere of open inquiry.

Team-planned (structured enrichment) curriculum appears in references to respective leadership, grade level, and departmental teams in improving programs of study in Chapter 4, to assumptions for existence of a planning team in the description of his naturalistic model for developing a new course in Chapter 6, and the approaches to adapting the curriculum in Chapter 7.

Student-determined (nonstructured enrichment) curriculum is targeted with achieving balance through content options of minicourses, integration through such broad-based courses as humanities, open access through ability grouping or curriculum tracking, and responding to student needs through the assessment process, school latitude, or homeroom meetings in Chapter 4. It also is expressed consistently starting with students for which the course is intended and focusing on quality of learning experiences in Chapter 6.

Glatthorn attends also to influences of the hidden curriculum, the impact of the organizational environment on what is learned. In this vein he places considerable faith on staff development. Glatthorn emphasizes the close relationship of staff development to curriculum development. It is the purpose of staff development to see that teachers possess the necessary skills for effective implementation of the curriculum. In fact, in Chapter 6, he considers staff development alone as a potentially viable approach to improving skills across the curriculum.

Even the loose-leaf format preferred for the curriculum guide is intended to offer teachers more flexibility and encourage them to develop a resource that is quite personal.

In Chapter 7 Glatthorn takes his audience into his confidence and his mind to explore emerging perceptions of a cooperative mastery model. The concept combines the strongest features of mastery learning with the effective components of cooperative learning while using the computer as an instructional adjunct.

The resources contained in the varied and comprehensive bibliography are themselves worthy of careful consideration.

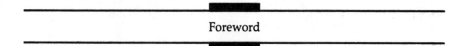
The book's content clearly excels on all six of Glatthorn's own criteria for evaluating a program of studies: goal oriented, balanced, integrated, skills reinforced, open-ended, and responsive. Its approach excels on all seven criteria for quality learning experiences: meaningful, involving, diverse, ethical, challenging, appropriate, and relevant.

Does this book tell you how to do curriculum? It most certainly does.

GERALD R. FIRTH
ASCD President 1986–87

Preface

I WROTE THIS BOOK AS AN "OPERATOR'S MANUAL" FOR EDUCATORS WHO have or hope to have leadership roles in the area of curriculum. It is very simply a "how to do it" book, intended to take the mystery out of the important task of doing curriculum.

Throughout the book I have used the first-person *I* for two reasons. First, I wanted to achieve a writing style that would communicate directly in the active voice and avoid the pseudo-scholarly third person. Second, many of the recommendations given come from my own experience. Wherever possible, I have drawn from the best available research, but in each case that research has been filtered through my own biases.

I also use the second-person *you* for two reasons. First, I wanted to speak directly to you, the curriculum leader who uses the book—not to some impersonal and indeterminate audience. And I hope to hear from you—about how you have used and improved on the processes described.

Although the work is thus in some ways personal, I also owe much to my colleagues. All the educators with whom I have worked have helped me test, refine, and sharpen my skills and knowledge. The graduate students at the University of Pennsylvania have challenged me to make these processes both more effective and more efficient. The executive directors of professional associations cited in the Appendix were very helpful in responding to my request for recommended sources. Ron Brandt first suggested the book and gave me valuable feedback as it progressed. I also wish to acknowledge the constructive critique I received from my colleague and friend, Dr. G. Michael Davis. And my wife Barbara was a never-failing source of support.

ALLAN A. GLATTHORN

1

How Do You Make Sense of All These Terms?

Curriculum and Instruction

The first concern is to understand the nature of curriculum and its relationship to instruction. That's no easy task. Even the experts can't agree on what *curriculum* means. Let me, therefore, provide a definition of curriculum that works for me—and explain how I see the connection between curriculum and instruction.

The curriculum is the plans made for guiding learning in schools, usually represented in retrievable documents of several levels of generality, and the implementation of those plans in the classroom; those experiences take place in a learning environment that also influences what is learned.

That sounds complicated, but its pieces make sense. *Curriculum*, as the term is used here, includes both the plans for learning and the actual delivery of those plans. The plans are usually presented in documents like guides and charts. The curriculum, broadly understood, also in-

1

cludes the *hidden curriculum*, the impact of the organizational environment on what is learned.

In this broader sense, curriculum includes instruction. That separation doesn't make sense to many educators who like to simplify things. In their view, curriculum is what is taught and instruction is how it is taught. The problem with such a separation is that it divides two entities that are almost inseparable. Almost all curriculum guides include suggestions for teaching—that is instruction. You really can't evaluate the curriculum without going into classrooms to observe instruction and what you see is the taught curriculum.

Levels of Curriculum Work

There are four main levels of curriculum work: curriculum policy, field of study, program of studies, and course.

Curriculum policy. A curriculum policy is a written statement of the rules, criteria, and guidelines intended to control curriculum development and implementation. Thus, if your school board has adopted a requirement that all high school students should learn about drug abuse, that is a part of its curriculum policy. Curriculum policy making is an important function; one expert points out that it is the "authoritative allocation of competing values" (Kirst 1983, 282). If your school board requires three years of science in high school but does not require any study of art, it has made an important value decision. However, because policy making usually lies outside the responsibilities of most curriculum leaders, it is not considered in this book.

Field of study. Mathematics, K-12, is a field of study. It is an organized set of learning experiences, usually embodying one of the standard disciplines, offered to students over a multiyear period. Thus, if you say, "Let's take a close look at secondary science," you are examining a field of study.

Program of studies. A program of studies is the total set of organized educational experiences offered for a particular group of learners over a multiyear period and encompassing several fields of study. Thus, if your school district is organized into three levels (and every school at a particular level has essentially the same program), then you have three programs of studies: one for the elementary schools, one for the middle schools, and one for the high schools.

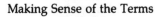

Course. A course is a set of organized learning experiences, within a field of study and part of a program of studies, offered over a specified period of time (such as a year, semester, or quarter) for which the student receives academic credit. The term *course* usually connotes a secondary school entity; elementary teachers tend not to think of courses.

These distinctions are important, as the rest of this book points out. You can't really answer the question "How do you do curriculum?" unless you specify the level. How do you improve the curriculum? That depends on whether you're talking about fields, programs, or courses.

Sorting Out the Types of Curriculums

In understanding curriculums, it helps to distinguish between these types: the recommended curriculum, the written curriculum, the taught curriculum, the supported curriculum, the tested curriculum, and the learned curriculum.

Recommended curriculum. The recommended curriculum is the ideal curriculum—what some scholar or committee thinks the curriculum should be. A good example of the recommended curriculum is the College Board's *Academic Preparation for College: What Students Need to Know and Be Able to Do* (The College Board 1983). It recommends very specific "basic academic competencies" and spells out the objectives of the "basic academic subjects." Recommended curriculums are useful as guidelines and hallmarks, but they usually ignore the realities of schools and classrooms.

Written curriculum. The written curriculum is the curriculum embodied in your district's documents—its scope-and-sequence charts, its curriculum guides, its program of studies booklets. It is the "official" curriculum of a school organization. In most cases the written curriculum is an instrument of control: It attempts to translate district policies and goals into documents that will enable teachers to implement those policies and meet those goals. Written curriculums are essential—but often they are not consonant with what is taught.

Taught curriculum. The taught curriculum is what teachers actually teach in the classroom. It is the curriculum that you would observe if you could sit there every day of the school year. As noted above, it is sometimes quite different from the written curriculum, despite the attempts of administrators to ensure congruence of the two.

Supported curriculum. The supported curriculum is the resources you provide to support the curriculum—the staff, the time, the texts, the space, the training. Although ignored in most curriculum texts, it is an essential element. You really can't do a valid evaluation of your foreign-language curriculum unless you take a close look at the supported curriculum. Which texts are you using? How much staff development are you providing? Which hardware have you bought? How much time is allocated?

Tested curriculum. The tested curriculum is the curriculum you see when you look at unit tests and final examinations. It is the measured curriculum.

Learned curriculum. That's the "bottom line" curriculum—what the students actually learn. It is the most important curriculum of all and is, in many ways, the one over which we have the least control.

One of the tasks of curriculum leadership, obviously, is to use the right methods to bring the written, the taught, the supported, and the tested curriculums into closer alignment, so that the learned curriculum is maximized.

Looking at Essentiality and Structure

The last set of concepts relate primarily to the written curriculum. In my own work with school districts, I have found it very useful to have them distinguish between these four kinds of objectives in the written curriculum: mastery, organic, team planned, and student determined.

To understand these four terms, work through the following steps with me, using any discipline you know well.

1. First divide that discipline or subject in terms of the essentiality of the objectives. Divide it into two parts—basic and enrichment. Let's call the basic part objectives that you think *all* students should learn. (*All* in this process means "all except the bottom 10 percent.") The enrichment part is what's left—the objectives that are nice to know but not really essential.

2. Now divide the curriculum in terms of its structure, making a distinction between the structured and the nonstructured. The structured objectives are ones that are best learned when they are carefully planned, specifically taught, and carefully measured. The nonstructured

4

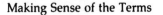

objectives are ones that do not require such careful planning, teaching, and measuring.

What you now have is a four-part division, shown in Figure 1.1. The *Mastery* curriculum meets two criteria: It is essential for all students, and it requires careful structuring. The mastery objectives might be seen as the "hard core" of the curriculum. They are the objectives that should be carefully sequenced and articulated. They require systematic planning and explicit teaching. They probably need the support of a good textbook. And they are easily quantified and measured.

The *Organic* curriculum is just as important, if not more so. It is basic for all, but it doesn't require highly structured organization, focused teaching, and careful measuring. The term *organic* is used to connote its main quality: It grows naturally with the right kind of nurturing. Thus, it might be seen as the "soft core" of the curriculum, containing the essential elements that do not require the systematic approaches of the mastery curriculum. In my view, the important affective outcomes of education are essentially organic. Here are some examples: appreciation of poetry, respect for other people, and a positive self-image. By analyzing a wide range of such organic outcomes, I have made a tentative determination that in general they are accomplished through two means. Some, like developing a positive self-image, are accomplished primarily through the class climate, through the day-to-day interactions in the

Figure 1.1. The Four Curriculums		
	Basic	Enrichment
Structured	MASTERY	TEAM PLANNED
Nonstructured	ORGANIC	STUDENT DETERMINED

classroom. Thus, a teacher interested in helping students develop a positive self-image would ensure that all had an equal opportunity to respond, all received the same type of response from the teacher for correct and incorrect answers, and all had an equal opportunity to succeed.

Other organic outcomes are nurtured through continuing instructional reinforcement: In planning the unit, the teacher keeps the organic outcome in mind and on every appropriate occasion reinforces it through discussion, explanation, or demonstration. Consider, for example, how an elementary teacher teaching science might nurture this organic outcome: "Develop a curiosity about the natural world." He or she might assign one pupil each week the task of writing on the board a "wonder why" question—something about the natural world that the youngster would like explained.

The *team-planned* curriculum includes enrichment, not basic content, but it requires careful structuring. The expectation is that departmental or grade-level teams will plan that component, so that there is no duplication from year to year. The student-determined curriculum is the unstructured enrichment part—the enrichment part that does not require careful planning but can be left to the emerging interests of the students in a particular class.

To illustrate these concepts, think about these three literature objectives for English-language arts, grade nine:

1. Define *theme*.
2. Appreciate short stories.
3. Explain the history of the short story as a literary form.

Most English teachers would identify the first objective as a mastery objective: It is basic and structured. Most would consider the second organic. It is basic—but you don't teach a lesson specifically on appreciation. You emphasize appreciation with every story that students read. Most would classify the third objective as team-planned: It is interesting but not essential; however, it does require careful planning. Now suppose in studying this unit, a student says, "I'd like to know how a television writer turns a short story into a TV drama." That becomes a student-determined objective, if the teacher sees fit to respond to it.

Making these distinctions is more than an academic enterprise; it has several practical advantages. First, it focuses district curriculum work on the mastery objectives, resulting in an uncluttered curriculum. As I'll explain more fully in later chapters, I believe that written district

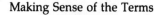

guides should be limited to mastery objectives; this gives the classroom teacher more latitude in emphasizing organic objectives and including enrichment content. It also simplifies the testing process: You test only the mastery curriculum. It also helps you make better decisions about textbooks: You choose texts for the mastery curriculum.

Making those distinctions also results in a more effective approach to the organic curriculum. Rather than placing an organic objective (such as "appreciating the value of mathematics in everyday life") at a particular grade level in a specific unit, the teacher is assisted in modifying the classroom climate and given suggestions for reinforcing the organic objectives whenever appropriate.

The folly of treating organic objectives in the same way you treat mastery outcomes is illustrated in one district's scope-and-sequence chart, which listed "listening courteously" as a second grade objective. That's not a second grade objective. It is an objective for every grade, for every unit, for every lesson.

These are the terms you'll need to understand in reading the rest of the chapters. If they don't make complete sense at this point, read on. They should become clearer as you use them in doing the curriculum tasks that follow.

References

College Board. *Academic Preparation: What Students Need to Know and Be Able to Do.* New York: Author, 1983.

Kirst, M. W. "Policy Implications of Individual Differences and the Common Curriculum." In *Individual Differences and the Common Curriculum*, edited by G. D. Fenstermacher and J. I. Goodlad. (Eighty-second yearbook of the National Society for the Study of Education, Part 1.) Chicago: University of Chicago Press, 1983.

2

How Do You Ensure That a School District's Goals Are Reflected in Its Mastery Curriculum?

Almost every school district has a set of goals. The goals are the very general outcomes you expect students to achieve after several years of schooling. Here are some examples of goals: think critically and creatively, become a good citizen, communicate effectively. In too many instances, however, goals are not directly reflected in the mastery curriculum. Instead, they are present only as implicit assumptions about desired outcomes—if they are present at all.

It seems to make good sense to relate most of those goals directly to the mastery curriculum. In fact, the research on effective schools

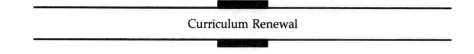

suggests a clear linkage between school goals and the curriculum. (See, for example, the reviews in Kyle 1985.) Making this connection explicit and direct is a useful way of operationalizing the goals. It says, in effect, "We take our goals seriously." It links the efforts of several departments in accomplishing a common set of outcomes.

There are many ways to achieve this outcome. One method that seems to work well is explained below. It outlines how a school district can relate its goals to its mastery curriculum. (Chapter Four explains how a slightly different process can be used at the school level.) And, as the last section of this chapter notes, the basic process can be modified in several ways.

The Basic Process Explained

1. Define your district's educational goals.

If your district doesn't already have a set of goals, get some goal statements that others have produced; then work with the faculty in modifying and adapting them for local use. Your state department of education probably has a set. John Goodlad (1984) has developed his own list, after examining goal statements from all of the states. Goodlad's list is a comprehensive—and the goals are clearly stated. I have developed a set for middle schools that you might want to examine (Glatthorn and Spencer 1986). And the ASCD book, *Measuring and Attaining the Goals of Education* (Brookover 1980), includes both a set of goals and subgoals and suggestions for measuring their attainment.

If the goals you start with are a brief list of general outcomes, you probably should amplify the list by developing several subgoals for each goal. The subgoals make the general goal clearer and provide some useful specificity. Here, for example, is how the ASCD committee analyzed the general goal of "self-concept" into several subgoals:

Goal Two: Self-Conceptualization
Subgoals
1. Recognizes that self-concept is acquired in interaction with other people.
2. Distinguishes between significant and nonsignificant others and their self-evaluations.
3. Takes into account significant others and disregards nonsignificant others in the self-conceptualizing process.
4. Distinguishes among many concepts of self in various roles or social situations.

5. Assesses own functioning in each of several different situations.

6. Perceives accurately, assesses validly, and responds appropriately to others' evaluations in the context of each specific role situation rather than generalizing to all situations (pp. 9–10).

How do you analyze goals into subgoals? You and a group of your faculty should take each goal, do some reading, thinking, and talking about it, and then answer these questions: "What subgoals make up this general goal? What is really involved in accomplishing this general goal?" Keep the list short—perhaps fewer than ten subgoals for each general goal.

2. Get faculty input in identifying the goals for the mastery curriculum.

This next step is an important one. Too many educators make the mistake of assuming that all educational goals are curricular goals. Thus, they worry unduly about how they can develop curriculum materials that will foster self-image. Now fostering self-image—like all the other goals of education—is a very important educational outcome. But it is probably best achieved through means other than the mastery curriculum. (Remember from Chapter One that the mastery curriculum is the district-determined curriculum that focuses on objectives that are essential for all students and require careful structuring.) You can foster self-image through the guidance program, through the extracurricular activities program, through other aspects of the organization (such as the school's discipline policies and practices), or through what I call the organic curriculum. (As explained in Chapter One, the organic curriculum includes all of the essential objectives that will be nurtured and fostered through the day-to-day classroom interactions between teachers and students.)

So you want to review your comprehensive list of educational goals and identify those that will be accomplished through the mastery curriculum. To do that, of course, you have to orient the faculty to what is happening and why it is being done. This orientation is probably best accomplished by sending out a memo something like the one shown in Figure 2.1 and then following up with school-based faculty meetings. The written memo ensures that everyone gets the same basic message, and the school-based meetings provide an opportunity for clarifying the process and getting teacher input. Notice that the memo avoids using

11

Figure 2.1. Sample Memo to Orient Faculty to Goal Project

We would like to inform you about our project to align our district's goals with its curriculum. As you are probably aware, the school board has officially approved the list of goals attached to this memo. Our next step is to be sure that those goals are connected with all aspects of our educational program—and especially with the curriculum, where that is appropriate.

To that end we have set up several K–12 subject-matter task forces. Each task force will be asked to identify which district goals its written curriculum will assume primary responsibility for and which ones it will contribute to. In accomplishing that important job, the task forces are encouraged to get input from all concerned faculty.

A district committee will then summarize and analyze the results of the task forces' work and will take further steps to ensure that all of our goals are being accomplished through some part of our complete educational program.

This project will be discussed more fully at a faculty meeting in the near future. Any questions or suggestions you have can be raised at that time. We believe that this is an important project and are interested in securing the cooperation and support of all of our faculty.

---

the terms *mastery* and *organic* at this stage in order not to confuse faculty or raise undue apprehensions. These terms can be explained later.

The next step is to set up several K–12 subject-matter task forces. You should have enough task forces to cover the entire curriculum. Thus, a typical district might have the following: English-language arts, social studies, mathematics, science, foreign language, health and physical education, and fine and applied arts.

Each task force is then asked to identify the goals that its mastery curriculum will be primarily responsible for or will contribute to, by using a form like the one shown in Figure 2.2. The task forces should be given ample quality time to complete their work and should be encouraged to get extensive faculty input. Impress upon task force members the seriousness of the task: Their responses are a commitment to the mastery curriculum.

3. Plug up the holes.

Now you have to plug up any holes revealed through an analysis of the task force reports. First, make a big chart like the one shown in Figure 2.3 (p. 14). Note on the chart the results of the task force surveys.

Then stand back and take a look at the results. First look at the r responses (denoting "primarily responsible for") and ask yourself these questions: (1) Is there at least one subject-matter area assuming primary responsibility for every subgoal? (2) If not, is it highly likely that that

---

Figure 2.2. Form Used by Subject Matter Task Forces

Tᴀꜱᴋ Fᴏʀᴄᴇ: *Social Studies, K–12*

    Listed below are the district's educational goals, along with the relevant subgoals. Think carefully about each goal and its subgoals in relation to the subject for which you are responsible. Then, by placing an *X* in the appropriate column, indicate for each subgoal whether your mastery curriculum will be primarily responsible for that subgoal, will make a contribution to that subgoal, or will not deal directly with that subgoal.

    In making this analysis, remember that the mastery curriculum includes only objectives considered essential for all students and that require careful planning and structuring. Also keep in mind that if you indicate your curriculum will be primarily responsible for or will make a contribution to that subgoal, then we will expect to find that subgoal explicitly reflected in your written curriculum guides.

Fᴏʀ ᴛʜᴇꜱᴇ ɢᴏᴀʟꜱ ᴀɴᴅ ꜱᴜʙɢᴏᴀʟꜱ	Oᴜʀ ᴍᴀꜱᴛᴇʀʏ ᴄᴜʀʀɪᴄᴜʟᴜᴍ ᴡɪʟʟ. . .		
	be primarily responsible for:	contribute to:	make no contribution to:
Goal One: Basic Skills			
1. Acquires information and meaning through observing, listening, and reading.	x		
3. Shares information and expresses meaning through skills of reflective thinking.		x	
4. Manipulates symbols and uses mathematical reasoning.			x

subgoal can be achieved through other means—through the organic curriculum, through the activity program, through the guidance program, or through other aspects of the school organization? (3) Or should we attempt to persuade one of the subject-matter groups to assume primary responsibility for this subgoal?

    In examining the sample returns shown in Figure 2.3, for example, you might feel a concern that no subject-matter group feels that its mastery curriculum should be primarily responsible for Subgoal 2, "acts as a self-reliant learner." That sounds to you like an important mastery curriculum outcome, and you aren't content to have it dealt with through those other means. So you decide to talk with the English-language-arts and science task forces to see if they are ready to accept this subgoal as a primary responsibility.

Figure 2.3. Summary of Task Force Reports

GOALS AND SUBGOALS	English-Language Arts	Social Studies	Mathematics	Science	Foreign Language
. . .					
5. Continuous Learning					
(1) Seeks and values learning experiences					
(2) Acts as a self-reliant learner	C	C			
. . .					

R = primarily responsible for
C = contributes to

Next take a look at the *c* responses (denoting "make a contribution to") and ask yourself these questions:

Are the subgoals appropriately reinforced across the curriculum? Or should we put pressure on one or more of the subject-matter groups to make a contribution to some of these subgoals?

Consider, for example, this subgoal from the ASCD publication: "Applies basic principles of the sciences, arts, and humanities to analyze and act upon public issues." What would you do if you found that the social studies department saw this as one of its primary curriculum responsibilities, but no other subject-matter group saw a need to contribute to it? You might well decide to talk with the science, arts, and English-language-arts task forces to sensitize them to the importance of contributing to that subgoal.

The manner in which you work with the task forces to plug up these holes will depend, of course, on your leadership style, the size of the district, and the organizational climate. The important matter is to be sure that all the critical gaps are filled.

4. Decide how you will accomplish goals and subgoals not reflected in the mastery curriculum.

Through this process you now should be able to produce a chart that shows each goal and its subgoals—and indicates which subject matter areas or fields of study are primarily responsible for and are contributing to those goals and subgoals. In a sense you have mapped the goal-based mastery curriculum, yet it is likely that there will still be some gaps. You and your faculty may have decided through this process that one or more of the subgoals will just not be dealt with through the mastery curriculum. If that is the case, then you have to decide how your schools will accomplish those subgoals. You really have four choices:

• We will accomplish this subgoal primarily through the organic curriculum—through the day-to-day teacher–student interactions. (This is a good choice, but you'll have to work at it through effective staff-development programs.)

• We will accomplish this subgoal primarily through the guidance program. (This is a legitimate choice if you have a very strong and comprehensive guidance program.)

• We will accomplish this goal through the activity program. (This is a legitimate choice only if all students participate in the activity program.)

• We will accomplish this goal through other elements of the organization. (This is a legitimate choice only if you specify those other elements and take the necessary follow-up steps.)

Once you have made those decisions, they should be reflected in a final comprehensive chart like the one shown in Figure 2.4. Down the left-hand side are listed all the goals and subgoals. Across the top are listed all the subject-matter areas and the four other means—the organic curriculum, the activity program, the guidance program, and other organizational elements. The letter r is used to indicate a primary responsibility, and the letter c, a contribution.

5. Disseminate the results and make plans for follow-up.

That final chart, with suitable explanations and interpretations, should now be disseminated to and discussed by the entire faculty. They should be given full opportunities to raise questions, to make objections, and

---

Figure 2.4. Final Mapping of All Goals and Subgoals

GOALS AND SUBGOALS	English-Language Arts	Social Studies . . .	Activity Program	Guidance Program
10. Participates in satisfying leisure-time activities	C	C	R	C

to offer suggestions, so that they feel a sense of ownership about the final product.

What practical use do you make of this final document? Its main purpose, of course, is to provide a general road map for school improvement. First, you may decide to give explicit attention to the nurturing of organic outcomes. The best way to accomplish this goal is through systematic staff-development programs that help teachers accomplish the following tasks:

1. Review, modify, and clarify the list of organic outcomes.

2. Determine which organic outcomes can best be accomplished by modifying essential elements of classroom climate. As noted in Chapter One, many organic outcomes are affected by climate—the structures and interaction patterns that affect interpersonal relationships. Thus, social studies teachers might decide that this social studies skill is related to classroom climate: "Participate in making rules and guidelines for group life." (The skill is one of several "group interaction skills" listed in a 1983 document published by the National Council for the Social Studies.) They would then discuss how students can be realistically involved in developing rules for their problem-solving groups.

3. Determine which organic outcomes can best be accomplished through continuing instructional reinforcement. As noted in Chapter One, some organic outcomes require continuing instructional reinforcement—the teacher remembers at every appropriate occasion to reinforce the outcome through brief explanation or discussion. Science teachers might identify this organic outcome for continuing reinforcement: "Recognizes the origin of science and understands that scientific knowledge is tentative and subject to change as evidence accumulates." (This is one of the attributes of a scientifically literate person identified in the 1982 position statement of the National Science Teachers Association.) They would then discuss together how such an understanding might be reinforced in every unit taught.

That document would also have value in improving a field of study. As explained in Chapter Three, such a list of goals is useful in systematically improving a field of study.

If you help teachers deal with organic goals through a staff-development program and use the mastery goals in a systematic improvement effort, then you should have left a small number of educational goals for which the activity program, the guidance program, and other organizational elements are primarily responsible. Because this book is concerned only with curriculum, it perhaps is appropriate here to describe only a general follow-up process for the noncurricular areas.

1. For each noncurricular area clearly delineate the goals and subgoals for which it is primarily responsible or to which it will make a contribution.

2. Assess to what extent that noncurricular area is achieving those goals and subgoals. Use surveys, interviews, observations, and other means to determine strengths and weaknesses.

3. Take steps to remedy identified deficiencies.

Delineating Mastery Goals through Other Methods

The process explained above is only one approach. The important concern is to be able to allocate educational goals to the several components of the educational program—or more simply, to produce a document that looks like Figure 2.4. The process described above proceeds by having subject-matter task forces looking individually at their curriculums, plugging up the holes, and then deciding how the noncurricular areas will take up the slack. The method seems to work because it is a bottom-up process that begins with the individual subjects and then moves to the whole program.

Obviously, however, you could reverse the process. You could start by deciding which goals and subgoals will be achieved through the mastery curriculum, which ones through the activity program, and so on. You then could take the mastery curriculum goals and subgoals and allocate those to the several subject fields. You could involve the entire faculty in making these decisions—or you could work with one small committee. There are many ways to achieve the desired outcome.

Do it in whatever way makes best sense to you. As long as you can produce a chart like the one shown in Figure 2.4 and have general faculty support and understanding, you're in good shape.

References

Brookover, W. B. *Measuring and Attaining the Goals of Education.* Alexandria, VA: Association for Supervision and Curriculum Development, 1980.

Glatthorn, A. A., and N. K. Spencer. *Middle School/Junior High Principal's Handbook: A Practical Guide for Developing Better Schools.* Englewood Cliffs, NJ: Prentice Hall, 1986.

17

Goodlad, J. I. *A Place Called School: Prospects for the Future*. New York: McGraw Hill, 1984.

Kyle, R. M. J., ed. *Reaching for Excellence: An Effective Schools Source*. Washington: U. S. Government Printing Office, 1985.

National Council for the Social Studies. *In Search of a Scope and Sequence for Social Studies*. Washington, DC: Author, 1983.

National Science Teachers Association. *An NSTA Position Statement*. Washington, DC: Author, 1982.

3

How Do You Improve Mathematics (Or Some Other Field), K-12?

I n this chapter you'll learn how to improve your curriculum in a given field of study. As explained in Chapter One, a field of study is usually defined as one of the standard subject-matter fields—like social studies, science, or mathematics—offered to students over a multiyear period. There are obviously many ways of improving a field of study, and the choice of a particular process is somewhat influenced by the structure of that discipline and how it is translated into sequences of courses. Therefore, the first part of the chapter explains the basic process, which seems to work especially well with subjects like English-language-arts, health education, and art, where the field is not divided into separate courses. The last part of the chapter explains how to modify the process for a field in which separate courses are offered, like secondary social studies (usually divided into separate courses called *American History* and *Political Science*) and high school science (usually divided into earth–space science, biology, chemistry, and physics).

A Rationale for a Consensus Curriculum

Before explaining the recommended process, it might be useful to offer some general guidelines about what such a process should look like. Doing so may help you think through your own modifications of the process recommended here.

1. Use a process that brings the recommended, the written, and the taught curriculum into closer congruence. Remember in Chapter One you learned about these three types of curriculum: the recommended curriculum, the curriculum that professional organizations and experts recommend; the written curriculum, the curriculum embodied in the district documents (scope-and-sequence charts and curriculum guides); and the taught curriculum, the curriculum actually being taught in your classrooms.

In too many schools, these three curriculums are often quite discrepant. The recommended curriculum seems not to have influenced the written curriculum or the taught curriculum; and the written curriculum is not fully reflected in what teachers teach. So you want a process that will bring the three into closer congruence—but you do not want a complete overlap. You want a written curriculum that reflects the best—but not all—of the recommended curriculum, because the experts don't have all the answers. And you want teachers to be giving primary attention to that written curriculum, while still having some autonomy.

2. Use a process that will result in a teacher-supported curriculum. The goal is to develop a consensus curriculum that teachers will want to implement because they have had a large measure of input in developing it and because they believe in its professional quality. This guideline is important because of what has been learned about the teacher as a curriculum maker. In general, the research yields the following composite picture. (The picture is drawn from several sources, chiefly Connelly and Ben-Peretz 1980; MacDonald and Leithwood 1982; Doyle 1986; Floden and others 1980; and Cusick 1983.)

> The teacher is an active curriculum maker who, day by day, makes important decisions about what is taught and how it will be taught; in making those decisions the teacher responds to numerous pressures and influences. The written curriculum plays a varying role in influencing teacher decision making—but at best, it is only one of several factors that the teacher considers.

Some have responded to this situation by attempting to develop stronger and more stringent controls over teachers to limit their influence on the curriculum. They hope in this fashion to mandate teacher compliance with the written curriculum. Such attempts seem doomed to failure: When teachers close the doors, they become the curriculum, regardless of all your efforts to make them behave differently. On the other hand, some have responded to the situation by simply tolerating it, either because they have an unrealistic view of the teacher's ability as a curriculum decision maker or because they value curricular diversity. Total diversity leads to anarchy—and tolerance of curricular anarchy does not seem to be a wise policy for the organization.

It seems more reasonable to use a curriculum-improvement process that will elicit active teacher support of a consensus curriculum—one that reflects their best judgment about what *should be* taught. Notice the emphasis on *should be*. You want teacher input, not about what they actually are teaching but about what they believe should be taught. The reason for the emphasis on the ideal rather than the real is that teachers know better than they teach. Their decisions about the curriculum typically reflect compromises they have made. They would like to emphasize other skills and concepts but, rightly or wrongly, believe that they are prevented from doing so—by administrators, by tests, by texts, or by subtle community pressures. So you want to use a process that will capture their best thinking about curriculum.

3. Use a process that will focus district efforts on the mastery curriculum. Remember that the mastery curriculum includes only objectives that are essential for all students and that require careful structuring. There are two main advantages for such a focus. First, it results in a kind of curricular parsimony—an uncluttered district curriculum that omits everything except structured essential content. Second, it explicitly provides for teacher autonomy in the organic, the team-planned, and the student-determined components.

The process explained below follows these guidelines. Feel free to modify it as you see fit.

The Basic Process Explained

1. Determine where you will begin and develop broad-based support for the project.

The first step is to decide where you will start with field improvement and to develop broad-based support for the project. Some districts develop a five-year schedule that ensures that, once every five years, each of the major fields and one of the so-called "minor" fields is reviewed. Others rely on a more formal needs-assessment process that uses a comprehensive assessment of district strengths and deficiencies. (For a useful survey of needs-assessment approaches, see Kaufman 1983.) Some simply monitor achievement-test scores to detect signs of trouble. Still others make intuitive judgments based on their knowledge of current developments in education and their informal assessments of curricular quality.

Regardless of how you decide where to begin, it is important, as noted above, to build broad-based support for the project. The teachers should be involved in whatever needs assessment or evaluations are conducted. If no formal process is used, then inservice time should be used to sensitize teachers to the importance of curriculum review and to solicit their support for and input into the process.

2. Establish project parameters.

The next step is to decide how comprehensive and ambitious your curriculum project will be. To do so, consider these questions.

1. How much time and money do we have? Limited time and money will make it necessary to take some shortcuts. The whole process can be simplified and accelerated. In my work with some districts with limited time and funds, we have been able to accomplish the entire project in as little as six months.

2. What grades will the project include? Usually it makes sense to develop the curriculum for all grade levels in which that subject is required. For example, if your district requires the study of art between kindergarten and grade eight, then the project should include K–8. You can handle the high school elective art courses separately, rather than including them in the comprehensive revision. However, you do not have to include all of the required levels in one project. In some districts where I have worked, we have begun with the high school curriculum and then worked on the middle school curriculum, since the elementary curriculum seemed to be in good shape.

3. How will the project provide for different ability levels? You have several choices here. One choice is to develop a separate curriculum for each ability level. A second choice is to develop a common curriculum for all students and train teachers in responding to individual differences. A third choice is a compromise between these two positions—

develop a common curriculum for the general population and then develop supplements for the less able and the gifted. (Chapter Seven explains some additional ways in which the mastery curriculum can be adapted so that it is more responsive to individual differences.)

4. What materials will be produced? Based on your assessment of the resources available and teacher needs, make a tentative decision about the kinds of materials you will produce. You may change your mind once you are into the project, but you should start with some tentative ideas. Here are the options:

• *A scope-and-sequence chart.* This is a basic document that will display in chart form what is emphasized from grade to grade. Although some districts manage without such charts, they are very useful in checking on articulation of content between levels and development of skills from grade to grade.

• *Curriculum guides or other materials for teachers*, to guide them in their own planning. These tend to be rather general documents organized by grade level.

• *Detailed units of study.* Detailed units of study including specific plans for instruction are sometimes needed, especially by inexperienced teachers. They are also useful when the curriculum is attempting to integrate content from more than one field of study or more than one area within a field (such as integrating speaking, listening, reading, and writing in language arts.)

• *Teacher-written learning materials for student use.* Some districts find it useful to develop model student-learning materials that teachers can then use in fashioning their own.

• *Curriculum-referenced tests.* Increasingly districts see the need for valid and reliable curriculum-referenced tests, to assist in aligning the curriculum and in assessing student achievement.

The process described below focuses on what seem to be the essential elements: the scope-and-sequence chart and the curriculum guides for teacher use.

3. Become acquainted with available materials in the field.

The next step is to collect and review the best available resources in the field. In doing this you are both developing your own knowledge base and accumulating resources for future use. Here are some of the materials you should gather.

• *State guidelines, requirements, and curriculum guides.* Analyze them closely to see how prescriptive they are and what help they can give you.

• *Exemplary curriculum guides from other school districts.* Most professional associations, including ASCD, provide for displays of such guides at their annual conferences. Such guides can give you some direction and some specific ideas for your own project. However, avoid outright plagiarizing. You want your guide to reflect your district's special needs and resources. If you do adapt any materials from other guides, be sure to ask permission and acknowledge the source in your publications.

• *Curriculum projects developed by nationally recognized professional groups.* Even though the days of buying and implementing "teacher proof" curricula are fortunately over, it still makes sense to examine the products of recent curriculum projects. If you find one that looks especially good, it might make sense to use it as the basis of your own work, involving your teachers in modifying it and adapting it for local use. In science and mathematics especially, where there seems to be a strong consensus among the profession about what should be taught, such adaptation might be a useful strategy.

• *Materials from appropriate professional associations.* Almost every professional association has produced curriculum guidelines for its field. As noted below, such materials can be very useful in the staff-development aspect of the project.

• *Textbooks and other instructional materials.* We all agree that the text should not determine the curriculum—but it does make sense to learn what the most recent texts are emphasizing. There is a caution, here, however. Remember that most texts are developed to sell in a national market. As a consequence, they make compromises. They leave out any potentially controversial content. And they repeat much content from grade to grade.

In the Appendix are some useful resources for both informing yourself and training your teachers. I have tried to include only materials that seem professionally reliable and are easy to use.

4. Orient and train the staff.

The next task is to conduct staff development to accomplish two goals: orient the staff about the nature and emphasis of the project and inform the staff about the best current thinking about that curriculum.

To accomplish the first is relatively simple. I have usually found that one carefully worded memo (something like the one shown in Figure 3.1) and one faculty meeting are sufficient. The ideas make so much sense to teachers that they ordinarily have no difficulty in accepting them.

The second task will require more time and effort. The intent here is to inform the teachers about current developments in that field, to give them an opportunity to discuss the recommendations of experts, and to help them reconceptualize the way they think about that subject. This last objective is important. There is a growing body of evidence that the way teachers think about a particular subject profoundly influences how they teach it. (See, for example, Gudmundadattir, Carey, and Wilson 1985.)

How do you accomplish this second task? First, review all the materials you have previously gathered and select those that seem to be most useful. Then disseminate those materials as background reading for what I call "staff development dialogs." (My thinking about these dialogs has been much influenced by Margaret Buchman's writings; see, for example, her 1985 article.) The intent of these dialogs is not to coach the teachers in acquiring a set of instructional skills; instead it is to help

---

Figure 3.1. Sample Memo Informing Faculty of Field-Improvement Project

To all elementary teachers and all secondary English-language-arts teachers:

We have decided to improve our English-language-arts curriculum, K–12, in order to update it and make it more effective. Your input about what should be emphasized grade by grade will play a key role in bringing about those improvements. To that end we will be holding a general faculty meeting about the project and some follow-up sessions about current developments in English-language arts.

One important feature of the project is that the district curriculum will focus on what we are calling the *mastery curriculum*. The mastery curriculum includes only objectives that are considered essential for all students and that require careful planning and structuring. In order to simplify our curriculum work, we will not include at this stage what we call the organic curriculum; that is, the essential learnings, chiefly in the affective domain, that should be emphasized on every appropriate occasion and do not require careful planning and sequencing. We also believe that all teachers should have a great deal of autonomy in deciding on the enrichment content of the curriculum, that is, learnings that are interesting but are not really essential. We believe that this focus on the mastery curriculum will give teachers greater latitude while ensuring that important outcomes are emphasized in every classroom.

We will have a faculty meeting on _____ to discuss these matters further, to answer your questions, and to solicit your suggestions.

---

them think about the subject they teach—and to think about it in a reflective and inquiring manner.

Here is the general tenor you wish to establish in these dialogs (and what you might say in a preliminary announcement and invitation):

> We are coming together to think about social studies and its place in our curriculum. We will be reading some brief reports summarizing the recommendations of experts in the field. The hope is that we will listen to those recommendations with an open mind. However, we will attempt to reflect about our own experiences as educational professionals—about what we have learned by teaching our students, in our classrooms. In the process we hope we can achieve a synthesis of the best of expert knowledge and our own lived experience.

In conducting these dialogs, you or a committee of teachers should read through the materials and identify four or five key issues in that field—the ones you consider most important from the standpoint of your faculty and your schools. Then take each of these key issues and proceed as follows.

1. Summarize the views of the experts about that issue.

2. Let teachers ask questions only to get greater clarity about what the experts recommend.

3. Ask each teacher to write a brief statement summarizing what he or she believes about that issue, based on the teacher's professional experience. These statements should be written prior to any discussion.

4. Have the teachers then meet in groups of five or six. Each teacher has a chance to read and explain his or her own statement. The rest of the group listen, ask questions, and respond briefly.

5. Each group makes a one-minute report to the large group. You listen closely to each report, limit each to one minute, and identify the extent of agreement and the source of disagreements.

6. Involve the entire group in thinking together about the major areas of disagreement. Don't push the group to premature and superficial agreement. If major differences exist, let them continue to be matters for further reflection and investigation.

7. Summarize the discussion.

The intent of these dialogic sessions is to create an atmosphere of open inquiry, not heated debate. The teachers first listen to the experts and are sure they understand before they differ. Then they work individually, so that each has an opportunity to discern and express a position, rather than having a few powerful members monopolize the discussion. Then they meet in small groups to listen to each other.

Finally, after that reflection, expression, and sharing, they come together to explore remaining differences.

Through this process they all will know what the experts recommend. They all will know what their colleagues believe about key issues. And many will have begun the challenging process of rethinking their subject matter.

5. Survey the teachers.

Now you prepare to "map the ideal," to learn from the teachers what they believe should be taught for mastery at their grade level. The first important task in accomplishing this goal is to prepare the form for the mapping step. The structure and quality of the form will very much influence the nature and quality of the results.

To begin the preparation of the forms, first develop a goal statement for that field of study. Remember that the goals are the very general long-term outcomes to be attained after several years of study, like "communicate effectively," "acquire the skills and knowledge for good citizenship," and so on. The goal statement lists two kinds of mastery goals: those that that field will be primarily responsible for and those that the field will contribute to. If you have used the process explained in Chapter Two, you can use the final chart you have produced as a basis for the goal statement. If you have not used that process, then you and a group of teachers, administrators, and supervisors should produce a statement that includes both types of goals.

The next step is to determine what strands you will use in mapping that field of study. The term *strands* is used here in the following sense: divisions of a field of study that are used in planning for learning over a multiyear period. The strands are the horizontal elements on a scope-and-sequence chart; taken together, they determine the scope of that field of study. Thus, I have identified these strands for English-language arts: critical reading and literature, speaking and listening, written composition, critical and creative thinking, study and information processing skills, and grammar and language study. (I usually recommend that beginning reading, spelling, and handwriting be handled separately.) Obviously, others would conceptualize English-language arts differently; however, those strands seem to have worked well in projects where I served as a consultant. It is apparent from this example that the way the strands are conceptualized will influence the kinds of data you get.

How do you identify the strands? Several methods can be used. In some cases the goals can be used to identify the strands. Look over the goal statement and decide whether the goals and subgoals will become the strands for that field or whether you will use other strands. The advantage of using the goals and subgoals as strands is that doing so ensures a close correspondence between the goals and the curriculum. The disadvantage is that the goals and subgoals may just not work well as curricular strands. They may not represent the way teachers conceptualize that field.

You can also check materials produced by professional organizations. Although such materials do not always use the term *strand*, they usually recommend several divisions of the subject. The materials listed in Appendix 1 should be helpful with the task of identifying the strands.

You can also identify the strands simply by exercising your own analytical powers, asking yourself, "What are the major divisions of this subject, as our teachers think about it?" For it is important in determining the strands to keep the teachers foremost in mind. Use strands that will make sense to them and that reflect how they conceptualize that field, even if their views are contrary to those of experts in the field. Also remember that the separate strands are only a planning tool. For example, the fact that I use a separate strand called "written composition" and one called "speaking and listening" does not prevent teachers from integrating speaking, listening, and writing.

With the strands identified, continue the development of the mapping forms. You will need a cover page explaining the whole project again. You will include the goal statement for that field. Then you will need a page or two for each strand. For each strand, begin by summarizing what the experts recommend. Then provide space for the teachers to indicate the general skills and concepts that they think should be emphasized for mastery in that strand, at their grade level. Figure 3.2 shows an example of such a form used in mapping social studies.

Before using the forms, ask a group of representative teachers to review them with these questions in mind:

1. Are the directions clear?
2. Do the strands make sense?
3. Are the recommendations of the experts clearly stated?

Those revised forms should then be used in surveying teachers' recommendations. However, the way that a survey is made makes a critical difference in the nature of the results. Rather than relying on a "mailbox survey," provide for quality time when teachers can ask ques-

---

Figure 3.2. Form Used for Mapping Social Studies

STRAND: SOCIAL STUDIES SKILLS   GRADE _____

TEACHER'S NAME _____   SCHOOL _____

IN PLANNING FOR THE DEVELOPMENT OF SOCIAL STUDIES SKILLS, THE
EXPERTS RECOMMEND THAT. . .

1. Skill development is an important aspect of the social studies curriculum. A skill
is the ability to do something well ("knowing how to").

2. Social studies skills are best developed through sequential instruction and practice, from kindergarten through grade 12.

3. The social studies curriculum should emphasize the important skills of *acquiring
information*: reading skills, study skills, reference and information-processing skills, the
use of the computer in getting information.

4. The social studies curriculum should emphasize the skills of *organizing and using
information*—critical thinking and decision-making skills.

5. The social studies curriculum should emphasize the skills needed for effective
interpersonal relationships and social participation—personal skills, group skills, and
social and political participation skills.

---

1. WHAT INFORMATION-ACQUIRING SKILLS DO YOU THINK SHOULD BE
TAUGHT FOR MASTERY AT YOUR GRADE LEVEL?

2. WHAT INFORMATION-ORGANIZING SKILLS DO YOU THINK SHOULD BE
TAUGHT FOR MASTERY AT YOUR GRADE LEVEL?

3. WHAT INTERPERSONAL AND SOCIAL SKILLS DO YOU THINK SHOULD BE
TAUGHT FOR MASTERY AT YOUR GRADE LEVEL?

---

tions about the project, discuss their ideas wlth each other, and take
time to think through these important matters. In announcing such a
meeting, ask teachers to bring whatever materials they think might assist
them in the task, for example, textbooks, tests, lesson plan books, and
professional articles.

In orienting the teachers at this meeting, stress the following points.

1. Each teacher is asked to recommend for *only one grade level*. Teachers who teach more than one grade level will, for the purposes of this project, be assigned to one particular level.

2. Teachers should focus on the *"mastery"* skills and concepts for that grade level. Listing a skill or concept for "mastery" at a particular grade level does not mean that we expect every student in that grade to fully master this skill or concept. It simply means that teachers will teach for mastery; that is, the skill or concept will receive systematic and thorough attention. Teachers should not indicate skills or concepts that they will only introduce or review briefly.

This point perhaps needs to be stressed. Many districts produce scope-and-sequence charts indicating when skills and concepts are introduced, when they are emphasized, and when they are reviewed. Such a chart seems unduly complicated. Instead, it makes more sense to me to develop an uncluttered chart that shows only when skills and concepts are emphasized. We make clear to teachers that they can introduce skills and concepts any time they think it appropriate—and they should review whenever necessary.

3. The separate strands are used for planning purposes only. Separating the divisions of a subject on a scope-and-sequence chart will not prevent teachers from integrating two or more of those strands, if that seems desirable.

4. Teachers should indicate only the *general* skills or concepts to be taught for mastery, not specific objectives. The specific objectives will be developed at a later stage. Teachers should not worry about how they word their recommendations; precision and clarity will also come later.

6. Collate and critique the results.

The next step is to collate and critique the results. A clerk with an hour of training can take all the returns, tally them, and display the results on a large wall chart or in a booklet. The chart or booklet should show grade by grade and strand by strand what the teachers recommended. (Returns can also show school-by-school results, if that seems important.)

Now you come to the critical juncture. You have to make some tentative decisions to reconcile the various recommendations of the teachers with your own best knowledge of what should be done. First, the teachers' responses will show that they often differ with each other about what should be emphasized. In general you want to be guided by what most of the teachers recommend, without simply letting a small majority rule. However, you also want to bring to bear the best critical judgment of those who have a deep and current knowledge of that field.

The best process for accomplishing both tasks is to convene a small group of knowledgeable supervisors, administrators, and teachers and to ask them to review the collated returns. As they review what the teachers have recommended, they should also be asking the following questions.

1. What important skills and concepts have been omitted and should be included?

2. What less important content has been included that might be dropped in order to reduce the content load?

3. What skills and concepts seem to be misplaced by grade level and might better be emphasized at some lower or higher level?

4. Is there good balance from grade to grade? Are some grades overloaded?

5. Does the scope and sequence at this juncture respond adequately to state mandates about student competencies?

6. Does each strand show a desirable development from grade to grade? Is there good progression in relation to difficulty and complexity? Are important skills and concepts reinforced from grade to grade when that seems appropriate (without excessive repetition)?

7. Does the scope and sequence adequately reflect the curriculum goals and subgoals for this field?

These last two questions perhaps need closer examination. Question 6 deals with the crucial issue of development and reinforcement without unnecessary repetition. To understand this issue, consider the matter of map-reading skills in social studies. How should the scope-and-sequence chart reflect adequate development and reinforcement without undue repetition? You have three choices here. You can show "map reading" as a general skill that will be emphasized at only one grade level—such as grade four—and then leave it to teachers in subsequent grades to build upon that foundation. Or you can use a "spiral" approach, noting it on the scope-and-sequence chart for grades 4, 7, and 11. Or if you believe that it should receive systematic and thorough attention at every grade level, then you note it for every grade level. If you make either of the latter two choices, then at a later point when

31

you develop specific objectives (see below), you can let the objectives reflect increasing difficulty and complexity.

Question 7 raises the important matter of linking goals with the curriculum. This question is critical, especially if the goals and subgoals were not used as strands. You simply take the goal statement and hold it against the teacher-generated results. If critical thinking is a goal, where does it appear in the scope-and-sequence chart?

By critiquing the results from these perspectives, the group should be able to develop a revised scope-and-sequence chart, one that represents the best synthesis of expert opinion and teachers' recommendations. That revised chart should then be submitted for teacher review, with appropriate explanations. If a large number of teachers raise strenuous objections to any element in the revised chart, you probably are wise to revise the chart accordingly. It makes more sense to develop a scope and sequence that has broad-based teacher support, rather than an ideal one that teachers will ignore.

7. Use the revised scope-and-sequence chart to develop grade-level objectives.

Now you have a revised scope-and-sequence chart, one that shows the mastery placement of general skills and concepts and that has broad-based teacher support. The next step in the process is to develop specific learning objectives based on that scope-and-sequence chart. The process explained below seems to work well here.

1. Appoint grade-level teams composed of skilled teachers who know how to write objectives. Give them the training and the orientation they will need.

2. Give them quality time to do the job and adequate compensation. I prefer to have teachers paid by the task, not the hour. "Get the job done any time and any place you can do it. It must be finished by August 1 and you don't get paid until your work has.been judged satisfactory."

3. Each grade-level team develops its own way of working together. Some may prefer to work together on all objectives. Others prefer to work individually, then critique each other's work.

4. Regardless of how they decide to work together, their task is the same: to take the mastery skills and concepts identified for each strand and turn them into appropriate grade-level objectives. The teachers decide, on the basis of their experience and knowledge, what are the attainable objectives for that skill and concept and for all students at

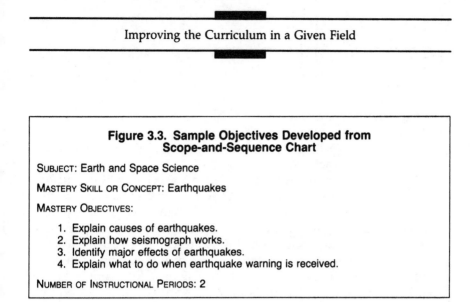

Figure 3.3. Sample Objectives Developed from Scope-and-Sequence Chart

SUBJECT: Earth and Space Science

MASTERY SKILL OR CONCEPT: Earthquakes

MASTERY OBJECTIVES:

  1. Explain causes of earthquakes.
  2. Explain how seismograph works.
  3. Identify major effects of earthquakes.
  4. Explain what to do when earthquake warning is received.

NUMBER OF INSTRUCTIONAL PERIODS: 2

that grade level. Figure 3.3 shows a set produced by a ninth grade science team. As the example illustrates, a small number of objectives is developed for each item on the scope-and-sequence chart. The wording is kept simple; there is no need to be as precise, as some measurement experts insist.

The results produced by each team are then reviewed by a subject-matter specialist, and appropriate changes are made. The expert checks to be sure that the objectives correspond with the scope-and-sequence chart, that they are clearly stated, that they are sufficiently comprehensive, and that they seem to be at an appropriate level of difficulty.

8. Package the results.

How much additional work you do from this point on will vary with the resources available and with your own perception of teacher need.

One choice, of course, is to produce the standard curriculum guide. Most guides include the following:
  • Rationale or philosophy.
  • Goals and subgoals for that field of study.
  • Scope-and-sequence chart.
  • Mastery objectives.
  • Teaching/learning activities.
  • Assessment and testing strategies.
  • Texts and materials.

My own preference is to produce a looseleaf curriculum notebook, which includes only the following:

- Goals and subgoals.
- Scope-and-sequence chart.
- Mastery objectives. (Each teacher gets objectives for the grades he or she will be teaching.)
- A summary of the research on effective teaching in that field.

I have found that such a notebook has several advantages. It is shorter and simpler, uncluttered with nonessential baggage. Instead of making specific suggestions for teaching each objective, it provides a general review of the research on effective teaching, giving the teachers much latitude about how they teach for an objective. And its looseleaf format invites teachers to add their own materials, for example, articles from journals, learning materials they have written or borrowed from some other teacher, or their own enrichment activities. In a sense, the notebook becomes their own personal curriculum guide.

9. Indicate curricular priorities by suggesting time allocations.

At some point in this process you should indicate curricular priorities by suggesting time allocations. Because the way instructional time is allocated significantly influences student outcomes, teachers need some guidance here. You have several choices as to when and how you do this.

Some districts find it useful to recommend the percentage of time that should be allocated to each strand, at each grade level, as in this example.

ENGLISH-LANGUAGE ARTS, GRADE EIGHT

Strands	Suggested Time Allocations
1. Critical reading and literature	25%
2. Speaking and listening	15%
3. Written composition	20%
4. Critical and creative thinking	15%
5. Study and information processing	15%
6. Grammar and language	10%

Those recommended percentages can be noted on the scope-and-sequence chart and also included in the curriculum guide.

A second possibility is to recommend the number of instructional periods that should be devoted to each set of learning objectives. Note that the example in Figure 3.3 handles time allocations in this manner. If you decide to develop detailed teaching/learning units, then it would be appropriate to include recommended allocations for each unit. Still other districts have developed very specific pacing charts that show week by week what teachers should be teaching. Although they believe that such pacing charts are a useful administrative tool, I believe that they are unnecessarily controlling.

However, this matter of time allocation is so important that it should be resolved through careful deliberation by administrators, supervisors, and teachers—not by imitating other districts or being influenced by my biases.

10. Follow-Up to Ensure Effective Implementation

Regardless of the kind of package you choose, you will still need to take care of some important follow-up responsibilities. You will need to be sure that valid and reliable curriculum-referenced tests are developed. You will need to choose basic and supplemental texts and the other instructional materials needed. You should provide additional staff development to ensure that teachers have the necessary skills.

Finally, of course, you need to be sure that the curriculum you have developed is actually implemented. Your chances of success will be significantly improved if you have worked out a systematic plan for implementation. Figure 3.4 (p. 36) identifies the important elements in such a plan; it is my own version of some excellent research-based recommendations offered by Fullan and Park (1981).

Modifying the Basic Process

There are several ways to modify this basic process, depending on the size of the district, the state of the present curriculum, and the nature of that field. As noted in the introduction, fields of study that are essentially collections of separate courses especially require a different process. Elective courses complicate the process still further.

Consider this example. Suppose your district offers a general science curriculum for K–8. In grades nine and ten students are required to take Earth–Space Science and Biology, respectively. In the last two years of high school they must choose one more science elective, either Chemistry, Physics, or Science and Technology. How would you handle such a complicated curricular array?

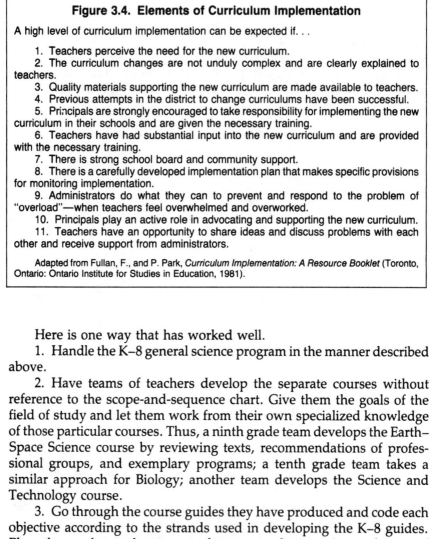

Figure 3.4. Elements of Curriculum Implementation

A high level of curriculum implementation can be expected if. . .

1. Teachers perceive the need for the new curriculum.
2. The curriculum changes are not unduly complex and are clearly explained to teachers.
3. Quality materials supporting the new curriculum are made available to teachers.
4. Previous attempts in the district to change curriculums have been successful.
5. Principals are strongly encouraged to take responsibility for implementing the new curriculum in their schools and are given the necessary training.
6. Teachers have had substantial input into the new curriculum and are provided with the necessary training.
7. There is strong school board and community support.
8. There is a carefully developed implementation plan that makes specific provisions for monitoring implementation.
9. Administrators do what they can to prevent and respond to the problem of "overload"—when teachers feel overwhelmed and overworked.
10. Principals play an active role in advocating and supporting the new curriculum.
11. Teachers have an opportunity to share ideas and discuss problems with each other and receive support from administrators.

Adapted from Fullan, F., and P. Park, *Curriculum Implementation: A Resource Booklet* (Toronto, Ontario: Ontario Institute for Studies in Education, 1981).

Here is one way that has worked well.

1. Handle the K–8 general science program in the manner described above.

2. Have teams of teachers develop the separate courses without reference to the scope-and-sequence chart. Give them the goals of the field of study and let them work from their own specialized knowledge of those particular courses. Thus, a ninth grade team develops the Earth–Space Science course by reviewing texts, recommendations of professional groups, and exemplary programs; a tenth grade team takes a similar approach for Biology; another team develops the Science and Technology course.

3. Go through the course guides they have produced and code each objective according to the strands used in developing the K–8 guides. Place the results on the scope-and-sequence chart, noting at the top of the chart the title of the course, not the grade level. If they have content that cannot logically fit into one of the existing strands, add a strand called "Special Mastery Emphases for Specific Subjects."

In reviewing the amplified scope and sequence to check on grade-to-grade progression, remember that the electives from which students will choose will probably not show a progression because they are not taken in a predetermined sequence.

References

Buchman, M. "Improving Education by Talking: Argument or Conversation?" *Teachers College Record* 86 (1985): 441–453.

Connelly, F. M., and M. Ben-Peretz. "Teachers' Roles in the Using and Doing of Research and Curricula Development." *Journal of Curricular Studies* 12 (1980): 95–107.

Cusick, P. A. *The Egalitarian Ideal and the American High School: Studies of Three Schools.* New York: Longman, 1983.

Doyle, W. "Classroom Organization and Management." In *Handbook of Research on Teaching* 3d ed., edited by M. C. Wittrock. New York: Macmillan, 1986.

Floden, R. E., A. C. Porter, W. H. Schmidt, D. J. Freeman, and J. R. Schwille. *Responses to Curriculum Pressures: A Policy Capturing Study of Teacher Decisions About Content.* East Lansing, MI: Institute for Research on Teaching, 1980.

Fullan, F., and P. Park. *Curriculum Implementation: A Resource Booklet.* Toronto, Ontario: Ontario Institute for Studies in Education, 1981.

Gudmundadattir, S., N. Carey, and S. Wilson. "Role of Prior Subject Matter Knowledge in Learning to Teach Social Studies." Paper presented at annual meeting of the American Educational Research Association, Chicago, April 1985.

Kaufman, R. A. "Needs Assessment." *Fundamental Curriculum Decisions*, edited by F. W. English. Alexandria, VA: Association for Supervision and Curriculum Development, 1983.

MacDonald, R. A., and K. A. Leithwood. "Toward an Explanation of the Influences on Teacher Curriculum Decisions." *Studies in Curricular Decision Making*, edited by K. A. Leithwood. Toronto, Ontario: Ontario Institute for Studies in Education, 1982.

4

How Do You Improve the Middle School's (or Some Other Level's) Program of Studies?

A s explained in Chapter One, a program of studies is the total set of organized educational experiences offered for a particular group of learners over a multiyear period and encompassing several fields of study. You are examining the program of studies when you ask questions like these: Should we give more time to science in the primary grades? Does our middle school curriculum respond to the special needs of young adolescents? Should we increase high school graduation requirements for our college-bound students? This chapter will suggest a process you can use to improve a program of studies.

An Overview of the Process

Obviously, many of these program issues have already been resolved for you. Your state has probably specified minimum time allocations for the various subjects. Your local board may have adopted curriculum policies delineating high school graduation requirements. And the K–12 curriculum guides in the different subject-matter areas implemented throughout the district control much of what is offered in a particular school. However, despite the number of policies and guides, you still have some latitude in shaping the program of studies for a given level of schooling or for a particular school.

Should each school at a particular level have its own individual program of studies—or should all schools at that level have essentially the same program? Obviously this is an important matter for boards and superintendents to decide. There are strong arguments for uniform programs in all schools at a particular level: Uniformity results in greater efficiency and probably a more equitable allocation of resources. And it is less likely that parents and the general public will make invidious comparisons between the schools.

On the other hand, there are good reasons for giving individual schools some latitude in shaping their own programs. There is some research suggesting that principals and teachers have a stronger commitment to their school's program of studies when they have had a considerable amount of influence in determining its nature. (For a cogent argument in support of school-based curriculum development, see the 1979 publication of the Centre for Educational Research and Innovation.) And school-generated programs would seem more likely to respond to the special needs of the students of that school.

A reasonable resolution of this dilemma would be for district leaders to require all schools to accomplish the district's educational goals, provide a uniform per-pupil budget for all schools at a particular level, and then give each school latitude in determining how it will achieve those goals for its pupils. The discussion that follows, then, assumes that schools have some latitude in determining their program of studies; however, the same basic process could be used on a districtwide basis.

First, take some essential preliminary steps.

1. Get the necessary approval and establish the needed mechanisms. Let the superintendent know that you intend to assess and improve the program of studies; assure him or her that no major changes will be made without going through channels. Set up a school-based

Program Improvement Task Force, a small representative group of faculty leaders and one or two members of the parent organization.

2. The task force should review the criteria in Figure 4.1 and discuss the issues implicit in each criterion. The criteria have been developed by reviewing the current literature on curriculum, by analyzing the criteria of accrediting bodies, and by reflecting on my own experience in helping schools improve their programs. I have attempted to identify criteria that are relatively free of any ideological bias, although my own sympathies are admittedly more liberal than conservative.

3. The task force should develop an assessment and improvement agenda. By reflecting about the criteria and by analyzing the present program of studies, the task force should identify criteria that seem to have special relevance for that school. Because these criteria deal with far-reaching issues and involve time-consuming processes, it makes sense to focus the improvement effort on perhaps two or three of the criteria that seem most critical. As will be explained below, most of the assessments require extensive faculty involvement, and most faculty have only limited tolerance for program-improvement efforts.

4. The task force should then develop a detailed implementation calendar, showing for each criterion the steps to be taken and the targeted completion dates. The steps to be taken are explained in the following sections; the dates can be determined by assessing the readiness

---

Figure 4.1. Criteria for Evaluating a Program of Studies

A sound program of studies is . . .

1. GOAL ORIENTED. The program of studies enables the students to accomplish the district's mastery goals.

2. BALANCED. The program of studies provides an appropriate balance between required courses that ensure mastery of essential knowledge and skills and elective courses that enable students to develop and pursue special interests; and the time allocated to those subjects appropriately reflects the school's curricular priorities.

3. INTEGRATED. The program of studies enables students to understand the interrelationship of knowledge and to use knowledge from several disciplines to examine personal and societal problems.

4. SKILLS REINFORCED. The skills required for learning in many subject areas (writing to learn, reading in the content areas, critical thinking, and learning and studying skills) are given appropriate and timely emphasis.

5. OPEN ENDED. The program of studies gives all students the knowledge and skills they may need for future success: Students are not tracked into dead-end programs on the basis of premature career choices.

6. RESPONSIVE. The program of studies is responsive to the special needs of the student population served by that school.

of the faculty and the resources available. This proposed implementation schedule should then be reviewed by school and district leadership.

5. The task force should provide continuing leadership in implementing the procedures, keeping administrators and teachers informed about progress and problems. So in the discussion below, when I speak about *you* taking certain steps, keep in mind that it refers to the task force working together under your leadership.

Aligning Goals and Program

Criterion 1: A Sound Program of Studies is Goal Oriented.

The program of studies enables the students to accomplish the district's mastery goals.

This criterion assesses to what extent the school's program of studies is consonant with the district's goals. There is some evidence, as noted in Chapter Two, that schools are more effective when goals and curriculums are aligned.

If you have used the process explained in Chapter Two to align district goals and the curriculum, then you can consider this criterion as met. However, if your district has not aligned goals and curriculum, then the following school-based process should work. You'll notice that it differs slightly from the district-based alignment process described earlier.

1. Identify the educational goals and the subgoals. If your district or school does not have a complete set of goals and subgoals, use the processes described in Chapter Two to delineate a complete set.

2. Work with the faculty to distinguish mastery curriculum goals from other goals. As explained in Chapter Two, all educational goals should probably not be accomplished through the mastery curriculum. Some should be accomplished through the organic curriculum, some through the guidance program, some through the activities program, and some through the organizational aspects of the school (such as its discipline policies and its reward system).

The best way to accomplish this important task is to meet with the faculty, explain the concepts of the mastery and the organic curriculum, and discuss how the non-curricular areas can make an important contribution to educational goals. With that background established, provide the faculty with a list of the school's goals and subgoals and ask them to put the letter *M* next to all the subgoals they think should be accomplished through the mastery curriculum. Remind them that this decision should not be made without due reflection: "An *M* means that we have translated—or are ready to translate—that subgoal into specific instructional units."

Then review the results of the faculty survey. Where there is strong faculty consensus, consider the matter settled. Where there is sharp division, discuss the issue with the faculty and make a decision that seems to reflect their preferences and your own considered judgment.

Through that process you should now have a list of the mastery subgoals—those general long-term outcomes that you and the faculty agree should be accomplished through the required structured curriculum. (Remember throughout this process that you are tracking only the *required* curriculum. Electives don't count because they are not studied by all students.)

3. Organize the faculty into subject-matter committees. Determine how many committees you will need by analyzing the size of the faculty and the number of offerings in the required curriculum. Here is how the committee structure might look for a medium-sized elementary school:

Reading and language arts
Social studies
Mathematics
Science
Art and music
Health and physical education

4. Provide quality time for each subject-matter committee to identify instructional units in their field that deal directly and substantially with the mastery subgoals. Direct each subcommittee to bring to the meeting such materials as curriculum guides, textbooks, and daily and unit lesson plans. Provide the subcommittees with a form like the one shown in Figure 4.2. (To save space, the form shown lists only one of ASCD's goals and its subgoals and shows entries for only two grade levels.) Ask them to indicate, grade by grade, the instructional units already in use that deal directly and substantially with the mastery subgoals. In doing so, they should write the title of the unit or a brief sentence indicating its main emphasis, like this: "How living things reproduce." Because many teacher seem to believe that all their units are accomplishing multiple goals, remind them of the meaning of the words *directly* and

43

Figure 4.2. Matching Units with Mastery Subgoals

SUBCOMMITTEE: Social Studies   SCHOOL: Lincoln Middle School

CHAIR: Kay Wiggins

GOAL: *Participation in the economic world of production and consumption*

Subgoals	Grade 6	Grade 7
1. Know career options	Geography and occupations	
2. Understand and value different occupations.		Culture and careers
3. Social and personal needs and careers		
4. Consumer decision making	Geography and consuming	Culture and consuming

---

substantially. You are not interested in identifying units that deal tangentially or superficially with the subgoals.

The committees should also list at the end of the form any units that do not seem to relate to any of the subgoals. One of the purposes of the alignment project is to identify units that might be dropped from the curriculum.

5. Collate and display the results on a large chart. List all of the subgoals down the left-hand side. Across the top list the grade levels and, under each grade level, the required subjects. Enter the titles or foci of the relevant units in the appropriate cells.

6. Determine what improvements are needed. By carefully analyzing the data on the chart, check for these two concerns:

• Is there any unnecessary duplication or repetition? Maybe the English-language-arts teachers and the science teachers both report they are teaching a unit in ninth grade on creative problem-solving. You have several choices here: Let them teach their own units, knowing they will present different emphases because of their backgrounds; encourage them to develop and teach a combined unit; or ask one of the departments to drop their unit or place it in another grade.

• Are there any gaps? You will probably find some gaps: Some subgoals are not dealt with at all, and some are not suitably reinforced from grade to grade or subject to subject. If the omission seems unimportant, simply note the fact. You might decide that a particular subgoal should not be dealt with at the level you are assessing. If the problem is more serious, decide what additional units are needed and where they should be placed.

7. Review the list of units that do not seem to relate to any of the subgoals. Meet with the teachers involved to determine for each seemingly unrelated unit whether it actually does deal with one of the subgoals, whether it should be modified to make it more goal relevant, or whether it should be considered an enrichment unit to be taught only if time becomes available.

8. Make the changes needed and bring the master chart up to date. Implement the decisions suggested by the foregoing analysis. Change the master chart to reflect any additions and deletions made. Make copies of the revised chart for the faculty, for district leaders, and for officers of the parent organization.

Achieving a Balanced Program of Studies

Criterion 2. A Sound Program of Studies Is Balanced.

The program of studies provides an appropriate balance between required courses that ensure mastery of essential knowledge and skills and elective courses that enable students to develop and pursue special interests; and the time allocated to those subjects appropriately reflects the school's curricular priorities.

This criterion is perhaps the most difficult of all to apply, for it involves subjective judgments about what constitutes "appropriate balance" and which subjects are most important. Predictably, there are sharp differences of opinion here. On the one hand, there are educators, like Theodore Sizer, who advocate a sharply focused curriculum that gives sole attention to the intellectual dimension of schooling. His prospectus for the "Coalition of Essential Schools" (1985) puts the matter this way:

The school should focus on helping adolescents to learn to use their minds well. Schools should not attempt to be "comprehensive" if such a claim is made at the expense of the school's central intellectual purpose. . . . The school's goals should be simple: that each student master a limited number of essential skills and areas of knowledge (p. 2).

At the same time, a large number of teachers and parents believe that the schools should offer a comprehensive and diversified program. Consider the evidence from John Goodlad's (1984) survey of parents.

Goodlad and his researchers asked parents how they would rate these four types of goals: intellectual, vocational, personal, and social. Their response was clear and direct: All four types of goals are "very important." Goodlad summed up the results this way: "We want it all."

There is some research to guide you here. Two scholars who carried out a retrospective analysis of transcripts and college entrance test scores found that students who completed the "new basics" (the more rigorous academic curriculum recommended by several reform reports) had considerably higher test scores than those who did not. (Alexander and Pallas 1983). However, my own (1986) review of the evidence suggests that that same rigorous curriculum might unduly penalize "at risk" youth. The research is generally consistent, however, in underscoring the direct relation between time allocations and achievement: The more time you allocate to a subject, the higher the achievement level. (See, for example, Berliner 1984.)

In the final analysis you have to rely on the limited research available, your own experience, your analysis of the needs of the students of that school, and your assessment of faculty and parent preferences. Here is a relatively simple but effective way of accomplishing the task.

1. Prepare a chart like the one shown in Figure 4.3. List all the required subjects, categorizing them in a way that will make most sense to the teachers. At the end of the list of required subjects, add the category "electives." Then decide how you will indicate time allocations: minutes each week, hours each week or total hours for the year, instructional periods each week, units of credit, or percentage of total instructional time available. Use a time allocation that will best help the teachers assess balance. My own preference is to report the number of 45-minute instructional periods for each week, although elementary teachers tend not to think about "periods." The important point is to be consistent and clear about how you indicate time allocations.

Then note on the chart the minimum requirements established by the state or the local district. Those entries will remind you and the teachers of the operating limits within which you will have to work. Then report what the experts recommend. To simplify this task I list in Figure 4.4 (p. 48) John Goodlad's (1984) elementary recommendations, my own recommendations for the middle grades, and Ernest Boyer's (1983) recommendations for the high school. (The elementary and high school figures represent my own interpretation of what Goodlad and Boyer seem to be recommending.) You may, of course, consult other

Figure 4.3. Assessing Program Balance

GRADES _____   SCHOOL _____

Subject	Required minimum requirements	Recommendations of experts	Our present requirements	Our desired requirements
English-Language Arts, Reading				
Social Studies				
Mathematics				
Science				
Foreign Language				
Health/Physical Education				
Arts				
Other requirements				
Total required				
Electives				

expert sources; the point here is to let the teachers know how some educational leaders have interpreted the issue of balance.

Then note on the chart your present time allocations. Now you have three sets of data displayed side-by-side: required minimums, recommended allocations, and present requirements. Leave the last "desired" column blank; you will complete that later.

2. Use the information on the chart as the basis for organized discussions with faculty and parents. Make the points that time is a limited resource and that time allocations seem directly related to achievement. Then ask the questions reflected in the criterion: Does our present program of studies have the desired balance between requirements and electives, and do our time allocations reflect our educational priorities? That general issue subsumes these specific questions:

- Are we giving enough time to the basic academic subjects?
- Are we giving enough time to subjects that nurture the aesthetic and the creative development of the learner?

47

Figure 4.4. Recommended Time Allocations

All time allocations are reported as number of 45-minute periods each week.

Subjects	Grades 1–4	Grades 5–8	Grades 9–12
English-language arts, reading	10	6	5 (for 2½ years)
Social studies	3	5	5 (for 3½ years)
Mathematics	7	5	5 (for 2 years)
Science	3	5	5 (for 2 years)
Foreign language	—	—	5 (for 2 years)
Health/physical education	3	3	2 (for 1 year)
Arts	5	3	2 (for 1 year)
Technology	—	—	2 (for 1 year)
Seminar on work	—	—	2 (for 1 year)
Senior independent project	—	—	2 (for 1 year)
Electives	2	8	16 (average each year)
Total periods	33	35	35

• Are we giving enough time to subjects that nurture the physical development of the learner?

• Does the program of studies provide the desired balance between required subjects and electives? Is there enough time for electives that develop special interests and talents?

At the end of the discussion, ask everyone present to complete the last column on the chart which asks for their recommendations about what should be done.

3. Analyze the responses on the chart and reflect on the discussions to determine whether there is strong support for any particular change. As you consider the options (lengthening the school day, increasing the time allotments to a particular subject, adding a subject, or changing the balance between required and elective courses), remember that major changes of this sort will have a significant impact on staff and budget.

4. Develop a specific proposal for changing the program of studies, providing a rationale for the change and analyzing the impact on resources. Present the proposal to the faculty for final review before asking for the superintendent's review.

If there is general agreement that students need more choices, consider whether *content options* might be useful here. I use the term to identify content choices within a required discipline or subject matter, to distinguish this kind of choice from deciding whether or not to take a subject. Content-option electives were popular during the early 1970s as 9- or 12-week minicourses. Thus, instead of taking English I, a student could choose from an array of courses with titles like Black Literature, Women in Literature, War and Peace, and Families in Fiction.

Although such content-option choices have been widely criticized (see Cooperman 1978, for example) as having contributed to the decline in SAT scores, they were never subjected to a rigorous evaluation. I am convinced that whatever weaknesses they did have were a result of careless design and were not produced just by giving students a choice of content emphasis. I have tried to show in another (1980) work and in the last chapter of this book that it is possible to design content-option electives so that they teach the important skills and concepts and are not intellectually flabby.

It would seem especially appropriate to consider content options for students in grades 7 to 10. Elementary teachers can provide content options in their self-contained classrooms without any fuss at all; and students in grades 11 and 12 preparing for college and a career probably need carefully structured courses that control content.

Achieving Curricular Integration

Criterion 3. A Sound Program of Studies Is Integrated.

The program of studies enables students to understand the interrelationship of knowledge and to use knowledge from several disciplines to examine personal and societal problems.

This is one of the perennial issues that divide the conservatives and liberals. The conservatives argue for the integrity of the disciplines: English is English, and social science is social science—and don't mix them together. Liberals respond by attacking "curricular fragmentation" and the "curriculum patchwork quilt." What is needed in the debate is enlightened deliberation, not sloganeering.

First, what does the research suggest? In general, it seems to support proponents of some kind of integration of knowledge. As you probably remember from your education courses, graduates of the experimental high-school programs involved in the Eight Year Study (with curricula that deemphasized the separate disciplines and maximized student choice) had higher grade point averages, received more academic honors, and were found to be more systematic in their thinking and more intellectually curious than their counterparts from traditional schools (Chamberlain and others 1942).

Also, a more recent review of the research on interdisciplinary courses concluded that interdisciplinary courses are as effective as separate-subject courses in teaching basic skills (Vars, 1978). Finally, there is some support for integration in the research on open classrooms, which typically emphasized an integrated curriculum. Although the conservative critics attacked the open-classroom movement as contributing to the decline in SAT scores, the research suggests otherwise. One recent and comprehensive review (Walberg 1986) concluded that students in open classes did slightly or no worse in standardized achievement and slightly to substantially better on several other important outcomes, (such as creativity, curiosity, and attitudes towards school. (The only exception was that students in open classrooms that were "radically" different from traditional classes did not fare so well.)

However, one other research finding must be noted here. Several reviews that have examined the effects of direct instruction conclude that in well-structured areas of the curriculum (such as beginning reading and mathematics), achievement is higher when the teacher presents a well-organized and explicitly focused lesson embodying the techniques of direct instruction (Rosenshine 1986). In general, the research suggests a conclusion of this sort: You may safely experiment with integrated courses as long as you keep your eyes on the basic skills.

Aside from the research, what else is there to guide you in deciding about the issue? There is a set of common-sense principles that might help you think about the differences from level to level.

1. In the earlier grades when pupils are attempting to master the basics, instruction that focuses on those separate skills is probably less confusing and more effective. Even if teachers use an integrated approach, they should provide focused instruction for the basic skills. Students learn to read by getting good instruction in reading and and by reading, not by discussing personal problems.

2. In the later years of high school, especially for students planning on higher education, some attention to the separate disciplines and their special ways of knowing is probably desirable.

3. In the middle school transition years, teachers can probably feel safer in experimenting with extensive integration. The basic skills have been mastered, and the need to learn the structure of the disciplines is less paramount.

4. Finally, it can be argued that all pupils at all levels should see the interrelationship of knowledge and should have an opportunity to examine issues that are not subject bound. You really cannot understand environmental issues unless you examine them from multiple perspectives: the natural sciences, the social sciences, and the arts and the humanities all make a contribution here. If you want to understand the nature of human conflict and how best people can manage conflict, what single discipline do you study? The answer is of course, not one but many: sociology, biology, psychology, history, philosophy, anthropology, and literature.

Obviously, I am arguing for an appropriate balance between integrated studies and focused attention to the separate disciplines. What is an appropriate balance? That key issue, of course, should be resolved at the local level. However, just to give you something to think about, let me present my own resolution of the issue.

Grades 1–4. Teachers in self-contained classrooms determine how much integration seems desirable, within limits established by the leadership team. At least five of the ten periods allocated to reading and language arts are set aside for focused instruction in reading; at least four of the seven mathematics periods are devoted to focused instruction. At each grade level teachers teach a minimum of two integrated units every nine weeks. Teachers cooperatively develop a scope-and-sequence chart showing the emphasis and placement of the required integrated units. Those integrated units draw primarily from reading, language arts, social studies, science, and the arts.

Grades 5–8. Teachers in multidisciplinarv grade-level teams determine how much integration seems desirable, within limits established by the leadership team. Of the six language-arts periods provided, at least two are devoted to focused instruction in writing, reading, and grammar. Of the five science periods specified, at least three are devoted to focused instruction in science concepts and skills. Mathematics is taught as a separate course. Teams are expected to teach at least three integrated units every nine weeks; they cooperatively develop a scope-and-sequence chart showing the emphasis and placement of the required integrated units. The integrated units focus primarily on social studies concepts and the developmental issues important to young adolescents;

51

they rely heavily on communication skills and draw additional content from literature, science, and the arts. If the study of a foreign language is begun, it is presented as a separate course.

Grades 9–12. Teachers work in departmentalized teams. In grade 9, English and social studies teachers jointly develop and implement a team-taught humanities course that draws primarily from the two disciplines and includes additional content from science and the arts. In grade 11, English and social studies teachers jointly develop and implement a team-taught American Studies course that draws primarily from those two disciplines but also gives significant attention to the arts. All other subjects are presented as separate courses.

I don't pretend that the above model represents an ideal resolution of the issue. It is simply my own attempt to define, level by level, the appropriate balance between integrated and focused studies in a way that makes some sense. It gives teaching teams authority to decide the issue, within general limits established by the leadership team. It recognizes the fact that the three levels are different in relation to the way that teachers can best work together. It recognizes that some disciplines are more easily integrated than others. And it acknowledges that separate subjects take on increasing importance as the student moves from level to level.

Finally, the model provides a framework for faculty resolution of the issue. At the elementary and middle school level, the following issues can be raised:

1. Do we wish to establish minimums for focused instruction? If so, what should they be?

2. Do we wish to establish minimums for integrated instruction? If so, what should they be? What subject areas should the integrated instruction draw from?

3. Do we wish to develop a scope-and-sequence chart showing the emphasis and placement of the integrated units?

I believe that at the high school level the issue should be posed as a decision involving "humanities" courses, defined for the faculty in this manner: Humanities courses are integrated courses that draw most of their content from English, social studies, and the arts. (Even though purists would object to that definition of *humanities*, it seems to represent the way most teachers understand the term.) In planning such humanities courses, you and your faculty should resolve these issues:

1. At which grade level will the humanities course be offered?

2. For which students will it be offered?

3. Will it take the place of existing courses or be added to the program as a new course?

4. Will it be required or elective?

5. How long should the course be: quarter, term, or year?

6. How many periods a week will it be scheduled?

7. What subject content will it draw from?

8. What organizing structure will be used?

The last issue perhaps needs some explaining. In general, humanities courses use one of the following organizing structures:

Area studies (American studies, Middle East cultures, etc.)

Aesthetic principles (balance, order, contrast,.etc.)

Cultural epochs (the Middle Ages, the Industrial Revolution)

Great works (great books, great works of art)

Major themes (war and peace, the nature of love)

Current issues (the environment, women's liberation)

These humanities courses enjoyed a wave of popularity in the 1960s and then experienced a decline in interest. However, there is some evidence of growing interest again. If they are well designed, carefully planned, and effectively taught, they can accomplish the goals of integrating two or more fields of study while giving the needed attention to important skills and key concepts. (Chapter Six illustrates how a humanities course can be developed in a way that integrates content from two or more fields and emphasizes some important "across the curriculum" skills.)

Improving Skills Across the Curriculum

Criterion 4. A Sound Program of Studies Is Skills Reinforced.

The skills required for learning in many subject areas (writing to learn, reading in the content areas, critical thinking, and learning and studying skills) are given appropriate and timely emphasis.

In a sound program of studies, separate subjects are strongly laced together with the key learning skills that cut across disciplines: All of the skills required for learning in many areas are given appropriate and timely emphasis. As I have analyzed the issue, it seems to me that there are four crucial sets of skills: writing to learn; reading in the content areas, critical thinking, and learning and studying skills. Because by their very nature these skills often fall in the cracks between the subject

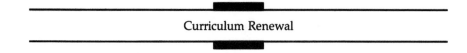
fields ("it's not my job to teach study skills"), the need to teach and reinforce them seems especially acute at the middle and high school levels, where the cracks are widest of all.

Because Chapter Five explains in detail a systematic and comprehensive approach to skill reinforcement, it is perhaps sufficient to note here that this issue requires examination. You should, therefore, meet with the teachers to look systematically at the following two issues.

1. Do we teach these four sets of skills systematically someplace in our program of studies? If not, where should they be taught?

2. Are these skills suitably reinforced in all subjects where their use is important? If not, how can they best be reinforced?

Achieving Open Access

Criterion 5. A Sound Program of Studies Is Open Ended.

The program of studies gives all students the knowledge and skills they may need for future success: Students are not tracked into dead-end programs on the basis of premature career choices.

This criterion focuses on the way the program of studies attempts to accommodate differences in students' abilities and aspirations. In examining this issue it is important to distinguish between *ability grouping* and *curriculum tracking*, a distinction often overlooked by many critics. Ability grouping tends to be of three main types. Ability-grouped class-assignment policies assign students to classes on the basis of their measured ability; thus, there is a top class, a middle class, and a bottom class. In within-class ability grouping, often used in self-contained elementary classrooms, teachers typically use flexible ability grouping: A pupil might be in the top reading group and the middle mathematics group. In regrouping plans, used in elementary schools, students are assigned to heterogeneous classes for most of the day and are then regrouped homogeneously for reading and mathematics.

The research on grouping by ability versus grouping heterogeneously tends to be somewhat inconclusive. In a comprehensive review of all major studies on the issue, two scholars concluded that ability grouping seems to have some slight advantage over heterogeneous grouping in relation to student achievement and attitudes (Kulik and Kulik 1982). For gifted students, they discovered, the advantage of ability grouping was even more pronounced. However, another synthesis by

Slavin (1986) of the research on grouping in elementary schools concluded that the research evidence refutes the belief that class-assignment ability grouping increases student achievement. Because the issue is so important and the research somewhat inconclusive, it makes sense for school faculties to continue to examine their grouping practices.

Curriculum tracking, on the other hand, is a practice of sorting students into different curriculum tracks based on career goals. Thus, it tends to be an issue especially relevant for high schools, which usually place students into one of three tracks: general, college preparatory, and vocational. Although several critics have claimed that curriculum tracking is chiefly determined by social class (poor students in the general or vocational tracks, middle and upper class students in college preparatory), a balanced and comprehensive review finds that the research on this issue is inconclusive (Rosenbaum 1980). The same reviewer found that the high school guidance counselor plays a key role in influencing a student's choice about curriculum tracks, helping students develop career plans and assisting them in choosing the particular track that will best serve those career interests.

Regardless of how students find themselves in different career tracks, the research strongly suggests that there are some serious problems with such tracking. (The findings below are all drawn from the Rosenbaum review, a review of the research that I consider to be balanced, objective, and comprehensive.)

1. Many students are in tracks that are inconsistent with career choices. They are not sure of career plans, have much misinformation about career requirements, and often change career plans soon after graduation from high school.

2. Once a student has been placed in a particular curriculum track, it is difficult to change. It is especially difficult to move up from general or vocational to college preparatory.

3. The specialized vocational and college preparatory curriculums do not appear to be providing effective preparation. This finding is perhaps so controversial that it would be useful to quote the reviewer's exact words:

Although observations suggest that some exemplary vocational curricula offer effective preparation, vocational curricula as a whole do not seem to lead to significantly improved outcomes. The college curriculum does show significantly greater success in getting students into college; however, this success may only reflect the deprivations experienced by students in other curricula rather than any particular accomplishments of the college curriculum (Rosenbaum 1980, 386).

4. Curriculum tracking tends to stratify the student body, creating many curricular, social, and time barriers to the interaction of students across curriculum groups.

5. Noncollege curriculums seem to be fostering a delinquent subculture: Students in the general and vocational tracks are more likely to report participating in such activities as drinking, smoking, playing truant, vandalizing, and gang fighting.

What should schools do in response to such negative evidence? Goodlad (1984) gives a strong and clear answer: Eliminate all curriculum tracking. Boyer (1983) offers what seems to be a more constructive solution: During the first two years of high school provide a common "core" curriculum for all students; during the last two years, devote at least half of the time available to "elective clusters," carefully planned elective sequences that would enable students to pursue advanced study of academic subjects or to explore career options—or both.

Although I find Boyer's proposal both sound and innovative, I realize that school leaders must deal with the reality that vocational–technical schools are deeply entrenched institutions, with their own vocal constituencies. I have seen enough excellent vo-tech programs that I am reluctant to abandon them simply because their graduates are not making more money than graduates of general programs. It would, therefore, perhaps make more sense for high schools concerned with the issue of curriculum tracking to undertake a program of incremental improvement in dealing with the tracking problem.

Under the direction of school leaders, high school faculties could consider the following issues.

1. When should students enter the vocational–technical school? Most experts I have read now recommend that the last two years of high school provide enough time for vocational–technical education. Some even suggest that one year of full-time study during the senior year might be sufficient.

2. Should we abolish the distinction between the "general" and the "college preparatory" programs? The division into these two tracks no longer seems justified. If the school is providing all students with a sound academic program in English, social studies, mathematics, and science, then counselors and teachers just have to be sure that students with any college aspirations understand the importance of studying a foreign language in high school.

3. How should we group students for instruction? Some grouping in mathematics and science probably is desirable. In English and social

studies, faculties might consider offering content-option electives, letting students sort themselves out. At the least, it seems wise to encourage the social studies department to use heterogeneous grouping, so that students of varied abilities and aspirations have an opportunity to exchange views about the past, present, and future.

4. How can we provide students with timely and useful career education? The best time for career education is probably the year before the student makes a decision about attending the vocational–technical school. You have several choices here about the delivery system for career education, for example, group guidance through the homeroom, a separate course, or a special unit in the English curriculum.

5. How can we improve the career guidance offered by our counselors? Guidance counselors probably need special training in career counseling to help them avoid these common mistakes: relying too much on single test scores, being unconsciously influenced by the student's social class and ethnic background, and directing students into vocational programs rather then helping students and their parents make their own informed choices.

A careful analysis of these issues should enable a faculty to develop its own program of incremental change to ensure that its program of studies opens, not closes, doors for its students.

Responding to Student Needs

Criterion 6. A Sound Program of Studies Is Responsive.

The program of studies is responsive to the special needs of the student population served by that school.

In thinking about and discussing this issue of a "needs-responsive program of studies," some parents and educators tend to take extreme positions. On the one hand, many argue that a school should provide a sound academic program and not concern itself directly with student needs: Any special needs, they contend, can better be met by other institutions—the family, the religious institution, the community. On the other hand, many contend that the development of a program of studies should be preceded by a complex and comprehensive "needs assessment" process; curriculum specialists should then develop the program of studies so that it responds directly and significantly to the needs thereby identified.

I advocate here a position somewhere between those two extremes. First, I believe that school faculties should have some latitude. To understand this point, contrast two hypothetical middle schools. Larchmont Middle School is in a conservative rural community. The community is strong, cohesive, and stable. Most families are intact and coping well. Local churches and synagogues have active and comprehensive programs for young adolescents. The Larchmont faculty, themselves somewhat conservative in outlook, decide that their program should emphasize academic preparation and not be directly concerned with the special needs of young adolescents. They offer a diversified activities program and a sound guidance program. They seem to have made a wise decision.

On the other hand, Lincoln Middle School is in a deteriorating urban community. The community is struggling, somewhat unsuccessfully, to deal with vandalism, drugs, and delinquency. The few churches and synagogues that remain seem moribund. Most families are headed by a working mother; most of those working mothers want the schools to help their children deal with the problems that surround them. When students attend school, the youngsters seem almost overwhelmed with their own day-to-day struggle to survive. The Larchmont faculty, generally liberal in their orientation, decide that their program of studies should deal significantly and directly with the problems the young adolescents are facing. They seem to have made a wise decision.

Second, even in situations where no other institution seems to be helping the young, I believe that only some part of the program of studies should concern itself with their special needs. A curriculum concerned solely with special needs can become trivial and boring: "Do we have to study teenage suicide again? We had that last year."

Finally, I believe in a reasonable approach to needs assessment. I find myself somewhat impatient with people who recommend highly complex and time-consuming needs-assessment processes that result in confirming the obvious: Our students need to develop a better self-image. It makes more sense, I believe, to use a relatively simple needs-assessment process that takes cognizance of the fact that most schools already have more data about their students than they use.

The process explained below, therefore, is intended to be a simple one that probes for needs not presently reflected in the program of studies and assesses to what extent students, parents, and teachers feel those needs should be reflected in the curriculum. The process assumes that you have a solid academic program with the elective balance you want. It also assumes that you are checking standardized and curriculum-based test scores to identify any serious problems with basic skills and concepts.

1. Prepare a survey form like the one shown in Figure 4.5. (p. 60). It has been designed so that it includes special student needs that are usually not reflected in the standard curriculum. The items have been worded so that they avoid using educational jargon. You may wish to have a small committee of teachers and parents review the survey form to be sure that it includes all of the items they consider important, that it does not include items that will create a storm of controversy, and that it does not include topics already in the curriculum that you wish retained.

2. Get the approval of the superintendent to conduct the survey. The superintendent in turn should brief the board, because the survey itself might become a matter of controversy in the community.

3. Set up a series of meetings at which the survey can be explained and questions can be answered. For parents, use a meeting of the parent organization. For teachers, use a faculty meeting. For students, use the homeroom time. The survey deals with such sensitive and complex issues that it probably should not be mailed out.

4. Analyze the returns. Assign weights to each answer: 3, *definitely*; 2, *maybe*; 1, *not*. Determine the mean response for each group and for the total group.

5. List the topics in order of perceived priority, as reflected in the mean total scores.

6. Present the results to the faculty. Help the faculty identify two groups of items:

• These items had a mean response of 2.5 or more from each group and should definitely be added to the curriculum.

• These items had a mean response of 2.5 or more from one or two of the groups. They will need further examination in order to determine the reasons for the differences in perception and to make a final decision about inclusion or exclusion.

7. Having determined the topics that should be added to the curriculum, meet then with a small task force to make a preliminary decision about how the topics will be added. You probably have the following choices:

• Add the topics to existing courses.
• Create one new course that includes all high-priority topics.
• Create a series of minicourses that can be offered throughout the year.

Figure 4.5. Assessing Students' Special Needs

YOUR ROLE: Teacher _____   Student _____   Parent _____

We are interested in getting your opinion about what special topics might be added to the school's curriculum. We want to be sure that the curriculum includes topics that are important to our students. Listed below are some topics that have been suggested. Consider each one. Then tell us your opinion about whether these topics should be added to the curriculum. Circle one of these answers:

Definitely: This topic should *definitely* be added to the curriculum.
Maybe: This topic *maybe* should be added, if there is time.
Not: This topic should *not* be added to the curriculum.

At the bottom of the page you may list any other topics that you think should definitely be added.

As you answer, keep in mind that if topics are added, then some present topics will have to be dropped or given less time.

The results of the survey will be used by the faculty in determining which changes, if any, should be proposed to the superintendent and the school board.

Topic	Your Opinion		
1. Avoiding alcohol and drug abuse.	Definitely	Maybe	Not
2. Learning how to be a good citizen.	Definitely	Maybe	Not
3. Making good moral choices.	Definitely	Maybe	Not
4. Learning about careers.	Definitely	Maybe	Not
5. Understanding how families are changing.	Definitely	Maybe	Not
6. Making wise decisions about sex.	Definitely	Maybe	Not
7. Learning how to be a smart consumer.	Definitely	Maybe	Not
8. Knowing how to prevent suicide.	Definitely	Maybe	Not
9. Protecting the environment.	Definitely	Maybe	Not
10. Preparing for college entrance tests.	Definitely	Maybe	Not
11. Improving our community.	Definitely	Maybe	Not
12. Making good use of leisure time.	Definitely	Maybe	Not
13. Understanding the future.	Definitely	Maybe	Not
14. Living in a nuclear age.	Definitely	Maybe	Not
15. Understanding the world's religions.	Definitely	Maybe	Not
16. Learning about world population control.	Definitely	Maybe	Not
17. Valuing our own and others' ethnic heritage.	Definitely	Maybe	Not
18. Reducing conflict between groups.	Definitely	Maybe	Not
19. Selecting and getting into the right college.	Definitely	Maybe	Not
20. Living in peace with other countries.	Definitely	Maybe	Not

If there are any other topics not listed above that you think should *definitely* be added, list them here:

21. _____

22. _____

23. _____

- Deal with the topics through carefully structured group guidance programs.

8. Prepare a proposal summarizing the data and explaining the curricular response you have chosen. Have the proposal reviewed by the faculty before submitting it to the superintendent for final review.

References

Alexander, K. L., and A. M. Pallas. *Curriculum Reform and School Performance: An Evaluation of the "New Basics."* Baltimore: Center for the Social Organization of Schools, Johns Hopkins University, 1983.

Berliner, D. C. "The Half-Full Glass: A Review of the Research on Teaching." In *Using What We Know About Teaching,* edited by P. L. Hosford. Alexandria, VA: Association for Supervision and Curriculum Development, 1984.

Boyer, E. L. *High School: A report on Secondary Education in America.* New York: Harper and Row, 1983.

Centre for Educational Research and Innovation. *School-Based Curriculum Development.* Paris: Organization for Economic Cooperation and Development, 1979.

Chamberlain, D., and others. *Did They Succeed in High School?* New York: Harper and Row, 1942.

Coalition of Essential Schools. *Prospectus.* Providence, RI: Author, 1985.

Cooperman, P. *The Literacy Hoax.* New York: Morrow, 1978.

Glatthorn, A. A. *A Guide to Designing an English Curriculum for the Eighties.* Urbana, IL: National Council of Teachers of English, 1980.

Glatthorn, A. A. "Curriculum Reform and "At-Risk" Youth." In *Re-thinking Reform: The Principal's Dilemma,* edited by J. W. Keefe and H. J. Walberg. Reston, Va. National Association of Secondary School Principals, 1986.

Goodlad, J. I. *A Place Called School: Prospects for the Future.* New York: McGraw Hill, 1984.

Kulik, C. L., and J. A. Kulik. "Research Synthesis on Ability Grouping." *Educational Leadership* 39 (May 1982): 619–622.

Rosenbaum, J. E. "Social Implications of Educational Grouping." In *Review of Research in Education 8,* edited by D. C. Berliner. Washington, D.C. American Educational Research Association, 1980.

Rosenshine, B. V. "Synthesis of Research on Explicit Teaching." *Educational Leadership* 43 (April 1986): 60–69.

Slavin, R. *Ability Grouping and Student Achievement in Elementary Schools: A Best-Evidence Synthesis.* Baltimore: Center for Research on Elementary and Middle Schools, Johns Hopkins University, 1986.

Vars, G. F. *Bibliography of Research on the Effectiveness of Block-Time, Core, and Interdisciplinary Team Teaching Programs.* Kent, OH: Kent State University, 1978.

Walberg, H. J. "Syntheses of Research on Teaching." In *Handbook of Research on Teaching* 3d ed., edited by M. C. Wittrock. New York: Macmillan, 1986.

5
How Do You Improve Critical Thinking (Or Some Other Set of Skills) Across the Curriculum?

As noted briefly in the preceding chapter, there are some important sets of skills that seem instrumental in the mastery of several disciplines. As I have analyzed the issue, it seems to me that these four sets of skills deserve special attention across the curriculum: writing to learn, reading in the content areas, critical thinking, and learning and study skills. Obviously, these four sets of skills are so closely related that it is difficult to sort them into separate categories, and others would probably group them differently. However, as this chapter will attempt to make clear, the four sets differ somewhat in how they can best be handled in the curriculum.

Regardless of how they are categorized, however, there is general agreement that these skills are fundamental in all academic learning and are not solely the province of one department. They also are not acquired naturally; they can best be mastered with systematic and explicit attention. If such skills are to be taught, reinforced, and applied across the curriculum, then you will need to do some careful planning. This chapter will explain a general approach you can use with all four sets of skills and then discuss some specific modifications useful for each.

A General Strategy for Improving Skills Across the Curriculum

Let's assume that the following conditions prevail: you have improved the fields of study so that they are reasonably up-to-date, and you have helped your teachers become aware of the importance of these broad-based skills in learning several subjects. How do you proceed to plan a "skills across the curriculum" project? The following strategy should be useful.

First, prioritize the areas for development. Although it might be feasible to strengthen all four skill areas at the same time, it makes more sense to focus on one area at a time and to accomplish that project before moving on to the next area. This one-area-at-a-time approach is less likely to tax material and personnel resources and will thus result in more effective curriculum work. In determining your priorities, consider these two central issues:

• What area represents the greatest need for your students? Do you have any data indicating that one of these areas is more critical from the students' perspective?

• What area will likely elicit the greatest teacher support? Do you have any information suggesting that they are more interested in one particular area?

Second, determine what levels will be included in the project. Although most districts would probably choose to plan a K–12 project, there are good reasons for considering some alternatives. First, it might be wise to limit the project to the middle and high schools. Elementary teachers in self-contained K–4 classrooms at times seem overwhelmed with too many demands: They are expected to teach the basic communications and mathematical skills, to teach science and social studies, and to help youngsters become socialized into the role of pupil. They also are probably integrating these skills in their own fashion and might see less need for explicit curriculum work in these areas. These two factors would probably make them much less receptive to a "skills across the curriculum" project.

Also, it might be apparent from your own evaluations that a particular set of skills is more critically needed at one level. For example, your evaluations might indicate that high school students were seriously deficient in academic writing skills.

Finally, decide which subject areas or disciplines will be included. The simplest way to resolve this issue is to decide that the four required academic areas will be involved—English, social studies, science, and mathematics. The rationale here is that these are the required subjects, and they make extensive use of all four sets of skills. A second approach is to involve all departments that express an interest. Thus, the art teachers might decide that they wish to participate in a "writing across the curriculum" project, while the industrial arts teachers decide to stress the reading of technical manuals. It is probably unwise to mandate the participation of all teachers, regardless of what they teach. Teachers of physical education who do not see any point in using writing as a means of acquiring motor skills will only waste their and their students' time in reluctantly giving attention to those skills. The other risk in requiring all teachers to emphasize writing or reading is that such an approach can have the effect of making the entire curriculum too verbal in its orientation. One of the special values of including subjects like physical education, art, and industrial arts in the curriculum is that they nurture and reward other kinds of talents.

Resolving these three issues should enable you to develop a planning chart similar to the one shown in Figure 5.1.

Finally, for the prioritized area, level, and subjects, determine through discussions with your teachers which general approach you will use to strengthen these skills across the curriculum. You have several viable choices here.

Figure 5.1. Planning for Skills Across the Curriculum Project

SUBJECT AREAS INVOLVED: English, social studies, science, mathematics.

GRADES	1989–90	1990–91	1991–92	1992–93
1–4	Studying			
5–8		Thinking		Reading
9–12		Thinking	Writing	

1. Staff development only. One approach is to let the written curriculum exist in its present form for the time being and place all your resources into staff development. The rationale here is that if you can train your teachers to integrate those skills effectively into their teaching, you will derive more immediate benefits than you would if you tried to change the written curriculum first. In a sense, the curriculum grows out of staff development: Informed and knowledgeable teachers write instructional materials reflecting the new approach, and those materials become an addendum to the existing curriculum. This emphasis on staff development, not the written curriculum, was essentially the strategy embraced by the highly successful National Writing Project.

2. Separate course. A second approach is to develop a separate course or sequence of courses dealing with that area. Thus, you might see fit to offer a separate course in thinking skills or in learning and study skills. Or you might decide to combine two or more areas into a separate course, like the following: Reading and Study Skills; Thinking and Writing Across the Curriculum. The arguments for and against the separate course are obvious. Those who advocate separate courses contend that such courses assure special and significant attention to the set of skills. Those who oppose the separate-course approach argue that such skills have a strong disciplinary component and are thus better learned within the context of that discipline. Unfortunately, there does not seem to be any significant research here to guide us.

3. Skill-intensive courses. A third approach is to identify certain required courses as "skill intensive" courses. At each grade level, certain of the subject areas are designated as courses where a particular set of skills will receive intensive treatment. You first identify the skill areas you wish to emphasize. Then you identify the required courses grade by grade where each area will be given special emphasis. In making such decisions, you weigh such matters as whether that course is required at a given grade level, the special developmental needs of the learners, the special nature of those skills, and the nature of each discipline or subject area. Thus, as Figure 5.2 indicates, reading skills might be emphasized in 9th grade science and in 11th grade social studies. You would provide some staff development to help 9th grade science and 11th grade social studies teachers teach content-related reading skills. You would also develop special instructional materials to assist them and make any needed modifications in the written curriculum.

The advantages of this approach are clear. It is a targeted approach that does not attempt to do too much. Neither students nor teachers are

Figure 5.2. Skill-Intensive Courses in the High School

SUBJECTS	READING	STUDYING	THINKING	WRITING
English		12	9	
Social Studies	11			12
Mathematics		10	10	
Science	9			11

overwhelmed with too much skill-focused instruction. And it attempts to find an optimal fit between the learning skills and the disciplines. The main drawback is that it can seem fragmented and piecemeal. Thus, you might fault the plan proposed in Figure 5.2 because it gives systematic attention to thinking skills only in two subjects at two grade levels.

4. *Selective emphasis.* The "selective emphasis" approach is a variation of offering skill-intensive courses. In the selective emphasis approach, the teachers in one particular subject area are expected to assume primary responsibility for teaching one of the sets of skills, such as study skills. Teachers in the other disciplines then give attention only to the special applications of those skills in their subject-matter areas. Thus, you might expect the English department to teach the basic skills required for academic writing; the science teachers would then build upon the work of the English teachers by showing their students how to apply academic writing skills in writing laboratory reports.

The advantage of this approach is that it assigns primary responsibility to one department, the one whose teachers perhaps have the greatest competence. The main drawback is that it can overload one of the departments—usually English—with "service" responsibilities. Most English teachers I know do not want to be seen as the "service" arm of the other departments; they value the integrity of their own discipline and do not view it as a "service" resource.

5. *Across-the-curriculum instruction and reinforcement.* In this last approach, you plan systematically to involve all of the disciplines in teaching and reinforcing the skill areas. The teaching of thinking, for example, is seen as everyone's responsibility. Each department is expected to develop its own special plans for teaching thinking, following general district guidelines. The advantage of this approach is that it is comprehensive. The main drawback is reflected in the aphorism, "What is everybody's job is nobody's job." Unless such plans are developed sys-

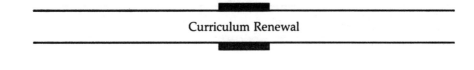

tematically and monitored effectively, they can result in teachers giving only minimal attention to the skills.

How do you decide which of the five approaches to use? Because there is not much research here, the answer depends upon your own careful analysis of the issue. Assess the attitudes and preferences of your teachers. Consider the special needs of your students. And, perhaps most important, analyze the special nature of the skills involved and how they may best be taught and reinforced. That topic is the focus of the rest of this chapter.

Using Writing to Learn Across the Curriculum

During the early 1980s schools seemed to give a great deal of attention to a movement commonly called "writing across the curriculum"—programs that attempted to help teachers use writing as a way of learning in the content areas. Although interest seems to have abated somewhat, it still makes sense to emphasize writing as a way of learning. The idea of using writing as a means of learning is grounded in sound theory, as two scholars (Yinger and Clark 1981) have noted. They advance these theoretical arguments in support of such programs: Writing is integrative, entailing the active use of one's total intellectual equipment; writing requires symbolic manipulation, which in turn facilitates learning; writing serves an epistemic function, modifying the human knowledge it records; writing is a unique mode of learning, involving all the major types of learning; writing provides both immediate and long-term self-provided feedback; writing is active and personal; and writing is a self-paced mode of learning.

Despite this theoretical soundness, there is not yet a conclusive body of research evidence that such programs either improve writing ability or improve learning in the academic disciplines. The mixed results of the studies conducted probably say more about the quality of the programs than they do about the soundness of the idea. My own review of several such programs suggests that they are much too narrow, focusing unduly on the writing of the term paper.

What would a sound program look like? A review of the literature on the teaching of writing and the nature of academic writing suggests that it might have the following characteristics. (For current and comprehensive reviews of the research on writing, see Hillocks 1986; and

Scardamalia and Bereiter 1986; for a sound treatment of the nature of academic writing, see Maimon 1983.)

1. Students would be taught how to apply the composing process flexibly. Although the experts seem to categorize the process differently, one formulation useful to teachers identifies five components of the composing process:

Prewriting: Finding a reason to write, finding a topic, analyzing the audience, gathering the information needed, developing a plan.

Drafting: Writing the first draft.

Revising: Changing major elements (adding new information, deleting, rearranging) to effect improvements.

Editing: Polishing the form.

Sharing: Sharing or publishing the results.

Unfortunately, too many teachers have applied the process inflexibly, insisting that students use all five in every assignment. Although the research suggests that such process elements as prewriting and revising are generally effective in most writing, there is now a growing realization that process models should be presented as alternative strategies to be used flexibly, depending on the nature of the writing task.

2. Students would be taught the basic skills useful in all kinds of academic writing. The following skills seem to be important: assessing the academic writing task and its demands; locating, paraphrasing, and storing information from secondary and primary sources; synthesizing such information in terms of the demands of the task; organizing academic discourse; writing fully developed and coherent paragraphs; substantiating assertions with appropriate evidence; using a style appropriate for academic discourse; using standard style manuals for matters of citation and documentation; using writing to demonstrate knowledge in academic contexts. (As I note below, even though I see these as identifiable skills, I believe they are best taught within the context of real writing problems.)

3. In each appropriate discipline, students would learn the ways of knowing and the forms of discourse especially important in that discipline. Thus, in social studies students would be taught the nature of causality as historians understand it and would learn to write about causal relationships in the way that historians write about them. They would then apply those special skills in responding to problem-centered writing tasks. In high school social studies, for example, they would write as young historians about the cause of some local event.

How do you translate these general guidelines into a specific curricular solution? Obviously, you have several choices. Let me outline one solution that I have found to be effective.

Because, as noted above, the literature suggests that there are both some common academic writing skills useful in all disciplines and some special skills unique to each, the "selective emphasis" model seems most appropriate here. English teachers would be expected to teach the basic skills of academic writing; teachers in all the academic areas (including English) would then teach the special skills and applications important in their discipline.

If such an approach seems useful, you would begin then by building academic writing into the English composition program, to ensure that all students learn to use the writing process flexibly and acquire and apply the basic academic writing skills. My own recommendation here is to include an "academic writing" strand in the English composition curriculum for grades 7 to 12. (Teachers in grades 4, 5, and 6 would teach the basic composing process and then introduce academic writing skills informally, without systematic instruction.) Here is how such a strand might look.

Grade 7: Summarizing and paraphrasing a secondary source.
Grade 8: Writing a paper based on two or three secondary sources.
Grade 9: Writing essay answers of one or two paragraphs.
Grade 10: Writing a paper based on three or more secondary sources.
Grade 11: Writing essay answers of three or more paragraphs.
Grade 12: Writing a paper based on primary and secondary sources.

For the most part, this conceptualization of the strand teaches the academic writing skills in the context of major writing problems, not in isolation.

Each department would then build upon this foundation, developing their own sequential array of writing problems that would reflect the special nature of writing in that discipline. In helping teachers from several school districts develop such discipline-based approaches, I have found it useful to have them distinguish between two ways of using writing as a way of learning: "continuing uses" and "special uses." The continuing uses involve the use of writing on an informal and continuing basis, perhaps several times a week. These continuing uses do not need special teacher attention; the continuing uses are identified simply to remind teachers that they probably use writing often as a way of having students record information, demonstrate knowledge, and respond to instruction. The list also serves to encourage teachers to use a wider array of continuing uses. Figure 5.3 lists the continuing uses that seem worthy of note.

Only the last two of these continuing uses perhaps need some explanation. First, many teachers have found it useful to ask students to keep an "intellectual journal" for that subject. In such a journal students record the following on a day-to-day basis: reactions to class instruction, questions about what is being learned, applications of subject-matter learning to their own lives, news reports about that subject, suggestions for topics that might be studied, and insights and reflections about the topic being studied. Second, many teachers ask students to write a response to clarify and fix what they have learned. This is not simply taking notes; it is an active construction of meaning through writing. "We've been talking a great deal about the Bill of Rights. Take a few minutes now to write a few sentences about what you understand the Bill of Rights to be—and why those rights are important in your own life."

The special uses of writing involve major assignments given perhaps only once every several weeks. (See Figure 5.4 for my own list of special uses.) They require carefully prepared assignments and special instruction for the students. The list of special uses serves to remind teachers that writing for learning is more than assigning term papers. The list also helps teachers in the several departments think about the important uses of writing in their discipline and make some decisions about where those types of writing can best be taught.

Here is how one science department used the list to develop a sequence of major writing problems to be taught and assigned each year:

Figure 5.3. Continuing Uses of Writing Across the Curriculum

1. Taking notes from teacher's lectures.

2. Taking notes from textbook.

3. Writing essay answers in tests.

4. Doing written exercises at home or in class to reinforce or apply what has been learned.

5. Keeping a journal for this subject.

6. Writing responses in class to clarify and fix learning.

Figure 5.4. Special Uses of Writing Across the Curriculum

1. Writing a report based on several sources.

2. Reporting the results of one's own investigations.

3. Describing one's own problem-solving or creative processes.

4. Writing a story, a poem, or some other type of creative paper based on this subject.

5. Writing about one's own response to or interpretation of a work in this field.

6. Explaining how this subject relates to one's own personal life.

7. Explaining to other students how to do some process important in this subject.

8. Solving a problem in this subject that requires the use of a special thinking skill and reporting on that solution.

9. Writing a persuasive paper on some controversial issue related to this subject.

Grade 7: Write a paper explaining how science relates to your personal life.

Grade 8: Write a report on some current science topic, using two or three secondary sources.

Grade 9: Write a persuasive paper on some current issue involving science.

Biology: Write a laboratory report.

Chemistry or physics: Write a report on some current science topic, using several sources.

If students learn the basic processes and skills in English class and then learn their special application in all the subject areas, they should learn to write better and learn more.

Reading Effectively in the Content Areas

For many years schools seemed seriously concerned about improving reading in the content areas. Now it appears that the interest in writing and thinking has taken attention away from reading as a way of learning. Such a development seems unfortunate, for reading plays an instrumental role in most academic learning.

As with writing, there seem to be some generic reading skills that are important in all the content areas and some special ones that are content specific. The generic skills listed in Figure 5.5 represent my own attempt to present in simple language the essential content-related skills

Figure 5.5. Skills in Reading Content-Related Texts

In reading content-related texts, the skilled reader. . .

Before reading:

1. Sets a purpose for reading. Decides on a purpose, formulates questions to be answered, and predicts the type of response that might be expected.
2. Calls to mind what is already known about the subject and attempts to learn any new terms that seem to be important.
3. Notes obvious features of the text (such as titles, illustrations, headings, previews, summaries, questions) and makes a tentative decision about author's purpose.
4. Makes predictions about the text—its organization, emphases, and probable difficulty.
5. Based on all the above information, makes tentative decision about rate of reading.
6. Monitors all of these prereading activities to be sure they have been carried out effectively and efficiently.

During reading:

1. Reads actively: evaluates what is being read for its importance and value, identifies and notes key ideas, makes inferences, guesses at meanings of words not known.
2. Reads flexibly: varies rate depending on importance and difficulty of passage, gives special attention to parts that seem important, skips over unimportant sections.
3. Reads constructively: relates what is being read to what is already known, elaborates on meanings by filling in the gaps, connects and relates parts to each other, makes personal sense of what is being read.
4. Monitors all these "during reading" activities to be sure that they have been carried out effectively and efficiently.

Immediately after reading:

1. Checks to be sure that questions have been answered; rereads to clear up any confusion or uncertainty.
2. Reflects about importance and significance of what has been read.
3. Systematizes what has been learned by making maps, matrices, lists, outlines, and other similar aids.
4. Monitors these "after reading" activities to be sure that they have been carried out effectively and efficiently.

Some time after reading:

Makes oral or written responses to what has been read:
1. Responds personally: makes personal connections with what has been read.
2. Reports what has been read: summarizes content and key ideas.
3. Interprets what has been read: explains inferences drawn, interprets important symbols and other elements, draws generalizations.
4. Evaluates what has been read: uses criteria to evaluate quality and value of what has been read.
5. Responds creatively: uses what has been read as a stimulus for own creative work.

that current theory and research suggest are important. (The following sources have been especially useful: Calfee and Drum 1986; Jones 1985;

Palincsar and Brown 1984; Paris, Oka, and DeBritto 1983; Tierney and Cunningham 1984.) You may wish to consult with the district reading specialist to generate your own list or to adapt some other. The important point is to be sure that you have a clear list of generic skills that teachers can use in teaching content-related reading. The research clearly suggests that these skills should be taught directly and thoroughly, not simply "mentioned." (See, for example, Gersten and Carnine 1986.)

Notice that the list is organized into four stages: before reading, during reading, immediately after reading: and some time after reading. The "some time after" category represents my own attempt to include in the comprehension model some recent theory about how students respond to literature. It includes five different kinds of oral or written responses.

To supplement this list of generic skills, the teachers of each department, working with the department chair or supervisor, should develop their own list of subject-specific skills. Because this task requires special knowledge of the discipline and the nature of its texts, it is a job best accomplished by subject-matter teams. To assist in this project, you may wish to provide them with copies of Figure 5.6, my own attempt to identify the important subject-specific reading skills that students

---

Figure 5.6. Subject-Specific Comprehension Skills

In comprehending texts used in this subject field, students should be able to . . . (and the questions teachers should be able to answer are . . .)

1. Interpret and use the special graphic aids often employed. (What kinds of graphic aids are typically used? How important are such aids as maps, graphs, charts, diagrams, and illustrations?)
2. Define and use the terms and concepts commonly used. (What terms and concepts are important and what special meanings do they have in this field?)
3. Identify the kinds of questions usually asked and use that knowledge to predict content. (What questions are usually posed and answered?)
4. Know the kinds of organizational patterns commonly employed and use those patterns to predict text organization. (What kinds of patterns are commonly used?)
5. Know the kinds of evidence usually provided to support claims and assertions in this field and use that knowledge to assess claims and assertions. (What kinds of evidence are usually provided?)
6. Identify the kinds of logical relationships often found in texts and understand such relationships when encountered in texts. (What kinds of logical relationships are often found? How important are these relationships: cause/effect, question/answer, comparison/contrast, classification/collection, description/attribute specification?)
7. Identify the types of bias sometimes found in texts and be able to detect such bias. (What types are commonly found, and how can that bias be detected?)

---

need to have and the corresponding questions that the teachers need to answer. I have found that asking departmental teams to examine their textbooks closely in order to answer those questions is a very useful staff-development activity. The activity forces them to confront some important teaching/learning issues in their own discipline that are often ignored.

Those lists of generic and subject-specific comprehension skills should provide an excellent foundation for a reading-in-the-content areas program. How do you incorporate them into the curriculum?

The first step is to decide about the scope of the program—what grades and what subjects? My own recommendation is to give systematic attention to content-focused reading in both the middle school and the high school—and to focus on social studies and science. Why only middle and high school? Elementary teachers can develop the basic reading skills and help pupils apply those skills to their textbooks on an "as needed" basis; there does not seem to be a need for a systematic program in content-related reading.

Why only social studies and science? The intent here is to focus the reading efforts in the two areas where the need is greatest. You can assume that English teachers will teach their students how to read literature. Teachers of foreign languages stress reading as one of the major components of the foreign-language curriculum. The need for reading in the fine and applied arts is so minimal that it seems unwise to give attention to those skills. You may need to give mathematics teachers some special help in teaching students how to translate word problems into mathematical formulations, but the teachers probably do not need an extensive program here. Social studies and science seem to be the areas where a special program seems most critically needed.

The next step is to decide which of the general models described above might be most effective in teaching reading in social studies and science. As noted above, this is an issue you can best decide. Because there are both generic and subject-specific skills, some combination of "selective emphasis" and "skill-intensive courses" seems most appropriate. The generic skills could be introduced and emphasized in the middle school reading program and then reinforced and extended in the high school English classes. With this foundation established, certain social studies and science classes could be identified as "reading skills intensive" courses. One pattern for sequencing is shown Figure 5.7.

With those decisions made, you would then proceed to develop the necessary supporting materials.

Figure 5.7. One Pattern for Teaching Reading in the Content Areas

SUBJECT	Grade Six	Grade Seven	Grade Eight	Grade Nine	Grade Ten
Reading/ English-language arts	Generic skills introduced	Generic skills emphasized	Generic skills extended	Generic skills extended	
Social studies		Reading intensive		Reading intensive	
Science			Reading intensive		Reading intensive

Developing Critical Thinking Across the Curriculum

In a cogent analysis of "common sense about teaching thinking skills," Beyer (1983) argues that four general research-supported principles for teaching skills have special relevance for designing programs to teach critical thinking. First, instruction should be systematic, moving through stages of readiness, introduction, reinforcement, and extension. Second, instruction should be direct: Introduce the skill; explain the specific steps; demonstrate; have students apply the skill in guided practice; have students restate and explain the skill. Third, instruction should be integrated with standard subject matter and with other skills like reading. Finally, instruction should be developmental, helping students become increasingly complex, abstract, and sophisticated in their thinking.

How can these four principles be applied in developing curriculums for teaching thinking? Let me outline one method I have used successfully that can be modified for your own district.

1. Begin by developing your own district list of *complex thinking processes* and *specific thinking skills*. The complex thinking processes are general mental strategies that subsume specific skills and are used in dealing with complex issues. Some examples of complex thinking processes are problem solving, information processing, and moral decision making. The specific thinking skills are more limited cognitive operations that can be used either independently or as part of a complex process. Examples of specific skills include comparing, classifying, and predicting. As one writer in the field has recommended, (Nickerson 1981) you and your teachers should decide which processes and skills you want

your students to learn and incorporate them into your curriculum, rather than adopting a taxonomy that some expert has proposed. In developing your own list of complex processes and specific skills, you may wish to modify the lists used in this chapter or consult one of the many other lists available. (My own lists of complex processes and specific skills are shown in Figures 5.8 and 5.11; other sources I have found especially useful are Cohen 1971, Presseisen 1984, and Brandt in press.)

2. Focus initially on the complex processes; they will be used in developing critical thinking units. Decide where each of those complex processes can best be incorporated into the required subjects. By conferring with supervisors and teachers and by reviewing the literature, determine which processes seem to fit each of the required areas of the curriculum. Your goal here is to ensure that each of the processes is emphasized in at least one—and preferably two—of the disciplines. The result of your deliberations should be a matrix similar to the one shown in Figure 5.9.

3. Work with supervisors and teachers in each of those areas to identify the topics of critical thinking units that would teach those complex processes. The critical thinking units are sets of 3 to 12 related

---

Figure 5.8. Some Complex Thinking Processes

1. *Controlled problem solving:* developing and applying algorithms and heuristics for solving convergent, closed, or controlled problems where there is one right answer.

2. *Inquiry and open-ended problem-solving:* identifying a problem, analyzing problem, gathering data, generating and evaluating solutions.

3. *Information processing:* framing a question, identifying appropriate descriptors, identifying appropriate sources, scanning and evaluating sources, recording and storing information, synthesizing and applying information.

4. *Reasoning:* recognizing assumptions, reasoning deductively, reasoning inductively, identifying fallacies in reasoning, using practical reasoning models.

5. *Evaluating:* classifying things to be evaluated, developing criteria and standards, applying criteria and standards, making and reporting judgments.

6. *Analyzing persuasive messages:* discerning persuasive intent, identifying and analyzing persuasive strategies, weighing well-intentioned persuasion.

7. *Mastering disciplinary inquiry:* understanding the special ways of knowing in that discipline, understanding the nature of "truth" in that discipline, understanding and applying the special methods of inquiry, understanding the uses and limitations of that method of inquiry.

8. *Making moral choices:* recognizing a moral issue, discerning one's core values, understanding the range of options, weighing competing claims, making a principled choice, evaluating choices.

9. *Using critical thinking in making life choices:* spending and saving, choosing a career, selecting a college, choosing a place to live.

Figure 5.9. Complex Thinking Processes and the Subject Areas

Processes	English-Language Arts	Social Studies	Science	Mathematics	Arts
Controlled problem solving			x	x	
Inquiry		x	x		
Information processing		x	x		
Reasoning	x			x	
Evaluating	x				x
Analyzing persuasion	x	x			
Disciplinary inquiry			x	x	
Moral choices	x	x			
Life choices	x	x			

lessons focusing on one or more of the complex processes. These decisions about the units should be systematized in a scope-and-sequence chart showing the grade placement and the specific focus of each unit. Figure 5.10 shows one such chart for English-language arts.

4. Collate all the information into a district scope-and-sequence chart showing the complex processes, the subject areas responsible, and the placement and focus of each unit. Review the chart to be sure that there is systematic development of the processes from grade to grade, that the placement of the units seems developmentally appropriate, that there is reinforcement without duplication, and that all required subject areas are suitably involved.

5. Provide the time and the resources for teachers to develop, field test, and modify the units.

By following those first five steps, you have developed units that will teach the complex processes. Now you turn your attention to the specific skills, using a somewhat different approach. In working with the processes, you began with a list of the processes and allocated them

Figure 5.10. English-Language Arts Thinking Process Units

GRADE	REASONING	PERSUASION	MORAL CHOICES	LIFE CHOICES	EVALUATION
5		Reading ads			
6					Evaluating products
7				Buying wisely	
8			Doing the right thing		
9	Logical errors			Career choices	
10		Propaganda			
11			Moral thinking		Evaluating literature
12		Language fallacies		College choice	

to the several disciplines. In working with the specific skills, you start with the subjects themselves, rather than with a list of skills.

6. Review with all of the teachers the specific thinking skills that might be important in their disciplines. I have found it useful at this stage to provide the teachers with the list shown in Figure 5.11. After reviewing the literature on critical thinking, I attempted to identify the key verbs that would communicate simply and directly with teachers. You should also, of course, review other lists of skills to be found in the references cited above and elsewhere.

7. After reflecting about the critical thinking skills, teachers would then identify specific thinking objectives that they wish to teach at particular grade levels, in addition to and outside the process units. To do so, they would review their textbooks, their curriculum guides, and the literature in their own field. Figure 5.12 shows a portion of one such list developed by a team of elementary language-arts teachers.

8. Systematize and review the reports from each team. Check for the following qualities:

- Do the thinking objectives appropriately reflect thinking skills?
- Do the objectives integrate content or other process skills?

Figure 5.11. Specific Thinking Skills

Directions: Below are listed some "thinking verbs"—verbs that suggest specific thinking skills. Use these verbs to help you identify thinking objectives in the subject you teach.

1. create
2. translate
3. classify and categorize
4. infer
5. synthesize
6. organize information
7. predict
8. interpret
9. determine cause
10. identify effect
11. evaluate
12. order and arrange in sequence
13. make analogies and metaphors
14. observe
15. identify errors and fallacies
16. compare and contrast
17. summarize
18. generalize
19. analyze
20. estimate
21. verify
22. conclude
23. memorize

- Are the objectives appropriately placed in relation to the cognitive development of learners?
- Is there appropriate reinforcement across the curriculum, without excessive repetition?
- Do the specific skills objectives avoid excessive duplication of content in the process units?

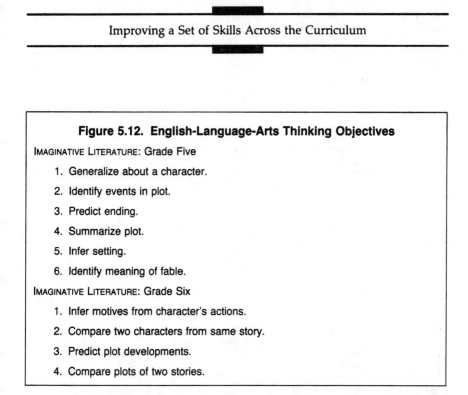

Figure 5.12. English-Language-Arts Thinking Objectives

IMAGINATIVE LITERATURE: Grade Five

1. Generalize about a character.
2. Identify events in plot.
3. Predict ending.
4. Summarize plot.
5. Infer setting.
6. Identify meaning of fable.

IMAGINATIVE LITERATURE: Grade Six

1. Infer motives from character's actions.
2. Compare two characters from same story.
3. Predict plot developments.
4. Compare plots of two stories.

At this point you now have a master list showing how the specific thinking skills will be handled grade by grade across the curriculum. Teachers will then need help in developing lessons based on those thinking objectives. Here I have found it useful to distinguish between *focused thinking lessons*, where the thinking objective is the main focus of the lesson, and *integrated thinking lessons*, where a content objective is the main focus, with the thinking skill simply noted and reinforced. Teachers can then use the approved list in their own lesson planning.

Helping Students Learn to Learn

For many years educators have stressed the importance of such study skills as taking notes from lectures and texts, preparing for tests, making efficient use of study time, and writing essay answers. In recent years researchers and practitioners have advocated a broader and more inclusive conceptualization that is not task specific and deals with learning in general, not just studying. Such a broader conceptualization is reflected in the list of "learning to learn" skills in Figure 5.13, which represents my own attempt to synthesize three very useful sources (Anderson and Armbruster 1984; Marzano and Arredondo 1986; Weinstein and Mayer 1986).

Figure 5.13. Learning and Studying Skills

1. Establish appropriate learning environment: arrange physical environment, allocate appropriate time.
2. Activate appropriate learning attitudes: interest in learning, sense of responsibility for one's learning, readiness to shut out distractions.
3. Analyze learning task and set learning goals: determine what will be required, how learning will be used, set specific goals.
4. Focus attention selectively in relation to goals.
5. Fix attention on important information: select it, store it in long-term memory, make it personally meaningful.
6. Use appropriate strategies to fix learning.
    a. Basic rehearsal strategies: repeat.
    b. Complex rehearsal strategies: copy, underline, make selective verbatim notes.
    c. Basic elaboration strategies: make mental images, make verbal connections, build associations.
    d. Complex elaboration strategies: paraphrase, summarize, create analogies, generate notes, write questions and answers.
    e. Basic organizational strategies: cluster, group.
    f. Complex organizational strategies: outline, make network, identify structural relationships.
7. Retrieve information from other sources and with other means (including the computer) to supplement immediate learning.
8. Store important information for future access: use computer, notebooks, journals, note cards.
9. Monitor entire process and make necessary modifications.

Regardless of how these learning and studying skills are conceptualized, educators have always recognized their importance. In fact, they are so important that the College Board (1983) identified "studying" as one of the basic academic competencies that all students should be expected to have in order to succeed in college.

How can these critical skills best be included in the curriculum? Again there are two separate issues here—teaching the general skills and developing the subject-specific ones. You first have to decide where you will teach the general skills. Here you probably have two viable choices in terms of the options described in the first part of this chapter: develop a separate course in "Learning and Study Skills" or choose reading/language arts for selective emphasis of learning and study skills.

In either case, you also have to decide when to teach the general skills. One solution here is to develop two courses or sets of "selective emphasis" units—one for the middle school, perhaps grade 6; and one for the high school, perhaps grade ten. In the middle school course or units, students would learn a simplified version of the general set of skills and acquire and use these learning strategies:

Basic rehearsal strategies
Complex rehearsal strategies
Basic elaboration strategies
Basic organizational strategies.

At the high school level, they would master a more complex version of the general set of skills, review the learning strategies previously learned, and acquire and use these new ones:

Complex elaboration strategies
Complex organizational strategies.

Once those general skills have been provided for, you next turn your attention to the subject-specific skills. Here the most effective approach is first to provide staff development for the teachers to ensure that they know the current theory and research on learning and study skills. With that background they can then identify the specific skills important in their subject areas and recommend when those skills will receive special emphasis. Figure 5.14 shows how one social studies department dealt with these issues.

You can then collate all the departmental reports on a large chart and review them with these questions in mind:

1. Are the skills placed at an appropriate grade level?
2. Are all the important skills included?
3. Is there sufficient reinforcement without excessive repetition?
4. Should adjustments be made in some grade placements in order to achieve closer correlation between departments?

Figure 5.14. Learning and Studying Skills Especially Important in Social Studies

SKILL	GRADE FOR SPECIAL EMPHASIS
1. Learn key concepts and terms.	All grades, 5–12.
2. Use computer to store and retrieve information.	5, 8, 11
3. Read and interpret maps.	5, 9
4. Interpret charts, graphs, time lines.	5, 9
5. Interpret political cartoons.	8, 11
6. Detect bias in visual materials.	11
7. Write essay answers.	8, 11

Deciding how to emphasize and reinforce all these complex processes is a complicated task, because you are dealing with skills that do not fall into neat subject-matter compartments. It may well be, however, that making these decisions in an insightful and productive manner is one of the most important curricular responsibilities you have.

References

Anderson, T. H., and B. B. Armbruster. "Studying." In *Handbook of Reading Research*, edited by P. D. Pearson. New York: Longman, 1984.

Beyer, B. K. "Common Sense About Teaching Thinking Skills." *Educational Leadership* 41 (November 1983): 44–49.

Brandt, R. S., ed. *Dimensions of Thinking*. Alexandria, VA: Association for Supervision and Curriculum Development, in press.

Calfee, R., and P. Drum. "Research on Teaching Reading." In *Handbook of Research on Teaching*, (3d ed., edited by M. C. Wittrock. New York: Macmillan, 1986.

Cohen, J. *Thinking*. Chicago: Rand McNally, 1971.

College Board. *Academic Preparation for College: What Students Need to Know and Be Able to Do*. New York: Author, 1983.

Gersten, R., and D. Carnine. "Direct Instruction in Reading Comprehension." *Educational Leadership* 43 (April 1986): 70–78.

Hillocks, G. J. *Research on Written Comprehension: New Directions for Teaching*. Urbana, IL: National Council of Teachers of English, 1986.

Jones, B. F. "Student Cognitive Processing of Text-Based Instruction: An Interaction of the Reader, the Text, and the Teacher." Paper presented at the annual meeting of the American Educational Research Association, Chicago, April 1985.

Maimon, E. "Maps and Genres: Exploring the Connections in the Arts and Sciences." In *Composition and Literature: Bridging the Gap*, edited by W. B. Horner. Chicago: University of Chicago Press, 1983.

Marzano, R. J., and D. E. Arredondo. "Restructuring Schools Through the Teaching of Thinking Skills." *Educational Leadership* 43 (May 1986): 20–26.

Nickerson, R. S. "Thoughts on Teaching Thinking." *Educational Leadership* 39 (October 1981): 19–21.

Palincsar, A. S., and A. L. Brown. "Reciprocal Teaching of Comprehension-Fostering and Monitoring Activities." *Cognition and Instruction* 1 (1984): 117–175.

Paris, S. G., E. R. Oka, and A. M. DeBritto. "Beyond Decoding: Synthesis of Research on Reading Comprehension." *Educational Leadership* 41 (October 1983): 78–83.

Presseisen, B. Z. *Thinking Skills: Meanings, Models, and Materials*. Philadelphia: Research for Better Schools, 1984.

Scardamalia, M., and C. Bereiter. "Research on Written Composition." In *Handbook of Research on Teaching* (3d ed), edited by M. C. Wittrock. New York: Macmillan, 1986.

Tierney, R. J. and J. W. Cunningham. "Research on Teaching Reading Comprehension." In *Handbook of Reading Research*, edited by P. D. Pearson. New York: Longman, 1984.

Weinstein, C. F., and R. F. Mayer. "The Teaching of Learning Strategies." In *Handbook of Research on Teaching* (3d ed), edited by M. C. Wittrock. New York: Macmillan, 1986.

Yinger, R. J., and C. M. Clark. *Reflective Journal Writing: Theory and Practice.* East Lansing, MI: Institute for Research on Teaching, Michigan State University, 1981.

6
How Do You Develop a New Course?

At some point you and your teachers may decide that a new course is needed. You may have decided that a separate course in one of the skills areas described in Chapter Five would be desirable, or you may have determined that an integrated humanities course would strengthen the existing curriculum. This chapter will review briefly the standard model for developing such courses and then explain in greater detail a naturalistic model that has been found effective.

The Standard Course-Development Model

The standard model is sometimes called a *technological model*, because it tends to be rational, systematic, and ends oriented. Its basic principles were perhaps most clearly explained by Ralph Tyler (1949); several recent works explain the process in greater detail and add a few special wrinkles. (Two good sources that I recommend are Posner and Rudnitsky 1982 and Wulf and Schave 1984.)

Because the technological model is so familiar, you probably need only a reminder about its basic steps.

1. Determine the course parameters: develop a rationale for the course, identify its general goals, and determine the time allocations.

2. Assess the needs of the learners: By reviewing test scores, by analyzing demographic data, and by surveying and interviewing, determine the learners' needs in the area to be covered by the course.

3. Determine course objectives: On the basis of the goals established and the needs identified, identify the course objectives.

4. Determine the sequence for course objectives: By analyzing the learners and the objectives, identify the optimal sequence for the objectives and cluster related objectives into unified learning experiences.

5. Analyze each objective to identify teaching–learning activities: Do a task analysis of each objective and identify the teaching–learning activities that will enable the learners to achieve those objectives.

6. Select instructional materials: Choose instructional materials that will facilitate the attainment of objectives.

7. Identify assessment measures: Determine how the attainment of those objectives will be assessed.

8. Organize all decisions and materials: Arrange them into a curriculum guide that will include the key components (the rationale, the goals, the objectives, the units, the teaching–learning activities, the instructional materials, and the assessment measures).

This technological model has several advantages. It seems orderly and systematic and, thus, can be readily mastered. It is efficient, because all the major decisions are made in relation to the outcomes. And it is often very effective, because it emphasizes the learning objectives.

However, it also has several disadvantages. First, it seems insensitive to the politics of curriculum making. Most curricular decisions are inherently political, because they involve matters of power and "turf." The process also seems to slight the importance of learning activities: Activities are selected only if they accomplish some predetermined objectives. Finally, the technological process does not reflect the reality of curriculum planning. As several researchers have noted, curriculum developers and teachers rarely plan in such a systematic, ends-oriented manner. (See, for example, Walker 1971 and Clark 1983.) For these reasons, some curriculum specialists have argued for more naturalistic models that would be more flexible and more interactive. (See, for example, Taba 1962 and Cohen 1974.)

A Naturalistic Model Emphasizing Quality of Learning

During the past few years, I have had some success in developing for and using with schools a naturalistic model that attempts to respond to the limitations of the technological model. My goal has been to develop a process that is sensitive to the politics of curriculum making, that places greater emphasis on the quality of the learning experiences, and that more accurately captures the flexible ways most of us plan for learning. I describe the process in some detail below, explaining how it might be used in developing an interdisciplinary humanities course for eighth graders. I strongly encourage you to try it out, add your own special twists, and let me know the results.

1. Stake out the territory.

This is a tentative and open-ended boundary-setting process in which you make some general decisions about students, schedule, and coverage. With your planning team, answer the following questions:
- For which students is the course primarily intended—which grade levels and ability groups?
- Will the course be elective or required?
- How long will the course last—a quarter, a term, a year?
- What weekly schedule probably seems desirable—how many times a week, how many periods?
- What will the course generally cover—what are the tentative goals for the course?
- Will the written course materials focus on only the mastery curriculum—or will organic and enrichment components be included?
- How will the proposed course relate to existing courses in the school's program of studies?

Your answers to these questions should be presented in a draft version of a course prospectus. The prospectus for the humanities course might read as follows:

We're thinking about developing a new humanities course for eighth graders tentatively entitled "Ordinary People." As we see the course now, it would be a required one-semester course, which all eighth graders would take instead of one term of their separate English-language-arts and social studies course. It would meet every day of the week, for a double period, which teachers could use flexibly. As we presently conceptualize the course, it would look at the history and culture of ordinary Americans, to give our students a somewhat different perspective about both the past and the present. It would include appropriate emphases on literature and the visual arts and would emphasize the skills of reading, critical thinking, and writing. All of these notions are very tentative; we need the advice of anyone competent and interested.

2. Develop a constituency.

The second step is to build political support for the proposed course. How much time and effort you spend on this second step depends on the extent to which the proposed course seems to have broad-based support. In developing a constituency, the following tactics seem useful:

• Win the support of the powerful. Be sure you have the support of gatekeepers like the school principal and the supervisor or department head.

• Respect the opposition. Listen and respond to the concerns of people who express some reservations about the course.

• Share the credit. Talk about the course as "our course." Open up the planning process to all who wish to participate. Spread the credit around.

• Be suitably modest. Avoid making extravagant claims for the new course.

• Be prepared to negotiate. Give yourself room to bargain—about length of course, space, staff, and budget.

3. Build the knowledge base.

Before beginning the development of the course, broaden your knowledge about the students, the teachers, the research, and other similar courses. Answer as many of the questions posed in Figure 6.1 as you can within the time available. The student questions will help you and your team understand the constraints imposed by the characteristics of students who will probably take the course. The teacher questions will help you decide how detailed your course planning should be and how much staff development you will need. The research questions focus on course content and teaching–learning methods. The "what's available" questions help you profit from the experience and work of others.

Figure 6.1. Questions to Answer in Building the Knowledge Base

THE STUDENTS: Consider the students likely to take the course and find out . . .
1. What is the IQ range?
2. What levels of cognitive development are represented?
3. What is known about their academic achievement?
4. What are their predominant values and attitudes relative to course content?
5. What similar courses might they have had before, if any?

THE TEACHERS: Consider the teachers likely to teach the course and find out . . .
1. How interested are they in teaching the course?
2. How much do they know about the content to be covered?
3. How skilled are they as teachers?

THE RESEARCH: Consider the course territory and find out . . .
1. What research is generally available that might help planners determine course content?
2. What research is available that will help planners select teaching-learning activities?

WHAT'S AVAILABLE: Consider the course territory and find out . . .
1. Have similar courses been developed by national curriculum centers?
2. Have similar courses been offered by other school districts?
3. What materials (texts, films, video cassettes, computer software) are readily available in the course area?

---

4. Block in the units.

Now you are ready to block in the units. You and the planning team need to make some tentative decisions about the number, focus, and sequence of the units in the course. In doing so, answer the following questions:

1. How many units of study will you probably need? Consider the goals of the course, the length and schedule of the course, and the interest span of the learners. Here is how the planners of the "Ordinary People" course resolved this matter.

If we have an 18-week course, we probably should plan for about 14 weeks, to allow time for organic and enrichment components. We'll be dealing with complex concepts and skills from two subject areas, so we'll need plenty of time. But 8th graders have a relatively short attention span. Let's tentatively think about five units of 2–3 weeks each.

2. What is the general objective of each unit? Identify the one general outcome desired at the end of the unit. It might emphasize a theme that ties the unit together ("understand how and why the American family is changing"), an overarching concept that includes several more specific concepts ("learn about communication"), or a general skill that embraces many behaviors ("learn how to spend money wisely"). Observe that at this stage the unit objective should be stated rather generally; you don't need precise language. Here are the unit objectives identified by the humanities team:

- Learn how and why the American family has changed.
- Learn how and why American leisure practices have changed.
- Understand how and why the nature of work has changed.
- Understand why religious practices have remained relatively stable.
- Understand how and why communication methods and media have changed.

Use those unit objectives to give a title for each unit: The American Family, Leisure in the U.S, Why Work?, Religion in American Life, Communication: Keeping in Touch Across the Decades.

Because determining unit objectives is a key step in the process, allow ample time to complete it. Ask the planning team to consider these issues: Which units will help students accomplish the goals of the course? Which units will appeal to student interest? Which units will be manageable within the time constraints? Which units do we think will be the most exciting to teach?

3. Determine the approximate length of each unit and the optimal sequence for the units. By reflecting about the unit objective and the nature of the learners, make a tentative decision about the length of each unit. Then determine the optimal sequence by answering these questions:

- Which unit will best capture student attention?
- How does the flow of units match the school calendar?
- Is some developmental progression desirable—does one unit build upon another?
- Which unit would make a strong ending, bringing several threads together?

Here is how the planning team tentatively resolved these issues about the "Ordinary People" course.

Leisure in the U. S.—3 weeks
Why Work?—3 weeks

Communication: Keeping in Touch Across the Decades—2 weeks
Religion in American Life—3 weeks
The American Family—3 weeks

5. Develop a unit-planning guide.

You have the units blocked out. Now you should develop a unit-planning guide—a general planning outline that can guide those who will be doing the detailed development. You can vary the form and content of these guides. Figure 6.2 shows one format that seems to have worked well for several planning and development teams. The unit-planning guide enables you to differentiate between two important levels of curriculum leadership: general unit planning and specific unit development. It thus facilitates the delegation of certain curriculum responsibilities.

6. Use the unit-planning guide to develop quality learning experiences.

Here is where the naturalistic model differs most from the standard technological model. If you were using the technological model, you

---

Figure 6.2. Unit Planning Guide

TITLE OF UNIT: The American Family

GENERAL UNIT OBJECTIVE: The students will understand that, although there are important elements of stability in the American family, certain changes have taken place and will probably take place. Those changes are a result of such complex factors as the nature of work, the economy, and shifting personal and cultural values.

LENGTH OF UNIT: Three weeks, 15 sessions, 90 minutes each session.

GENERAL SUGGESTIONS ABOUT SHAPING THE UNIT: It probably would be best to divide the unit into three parts, roughly one week for each: the family, 1920–1930; the family, 1980–1990; the family, 2010–2020.

IMPORTANT CONCEPTS TO BE LEARNED:
    1. From social studies: family, nuclear family, extended family, patriarchal family.
    2. From English-language arts: theme.

IMPORTANT SKILLS TO BE DEVELOPED:
    1. Critical thinking: comparing and contrasting, identifying causes, predicting.
    2. Reading in the content areas: summarizing, identifying themes.
    3. Writing across the curriculum: writing a futuristic short story.

---

would next identify the specific learning objectives for each of the units and then suggest learning experiences and materials that would enable students to accomplish those learning experiences. In the naturalistic model, you and your team attempt to design quality learning experiences by beginning at any point in the process. You may begin by thinking about objectives. More likely you will start by thinking of stimulating learning activities or excellent materials. Here is the way to develop quality learning experiences.

1. Orient the development teams to the nature of quality learning experiences. Such experiences should meet seven criteria. Those criteria are listed in Figure 6.3, so that they can be reproduced and disseminated readily.

2. With these criteria in mind, the development teams review the unit-planning guide and use a group problem-solving process (such as brainstorming) to tentatively identify several quality learning experiences—more than they will probably need. They think of stimulating activities and experiences. They identify interesting materials. They do not worry unduly about specific objectives at this stage, unless they find it helpful to do so. In the initial planning stage, they do not concern themselves with sequence; instead they focus on quality learning. Figure 6.4 shows one such list that might be developed for the last part of the "American Family" unit.

Figure 6.3. Criteria for Quality Learning Experiences

1. The learning experience is meaningful. It provides an opportunity for students to discover meaning, to make sense of their experience, to integrate knowledge.
2. The learning experience is involving. Its nature is such that it seems likely to involve all students in the active processing of experience.
3. The learning experience is diverse and multiple. It requires the use of many learning styles, modalities, and talents.
4. The learning experience is ethical. It does not require the use of deception by students or teachers and in no way diminishes the dignity of participants.
5. The learning experience is challenging. It requires the students to acquire new information and also to process that information: to synthesize it, apply it, and create new forms.
6. The learning experience is appropriate. It is appropriate for the context (the classroom or the community) and the participants (the teachers and the students).
7. The learning experience is relevant. It relates to and contributes to the unit objective.

Figure 6.4. Quality Learning Experiences: The American Family

GENERAL FOCUS OF THE EXPERIENCES: The students will realize that the American family will probably change in some ways by the year 2010; although all changes are probably not predictable, some are more likely than others.

SUGGESTED QUALITY LEARNING EXPERIENCES:

1. Dramatize part of B. F. Skinner's *Walden Two* and discuss how desirable his utopian ideas about community are—and whether there is any likelihood that they might be realized. (This might be a good place to teach the concept of *theme*. Also, students who are artistically talented should be encouraged to illustrate the novel's setting. More able students also may wish to read the attacks of some critics who disagreed strongly with Skinner's vision.)

2. Interview (by telephone perhaps) a member of a contemporary "Utopian" community. (Be sure to teach interviewing skills—preparing questions, listening to answers, recording answers, following up on answers. If time is available and students are interested, teach them how to report the results of an interview.)

3. Read an account of the successes and failures of one of the "utopian" communities that started in the late 1960s. (This would be a good place to teach and apply the summarizing skill.)

4. Identify through discussion the chief factors that will probably affect the American family in the year 2010: the computer and its effects on working and communicating; new methods of population control; the move towards multiple-income families; new opportunities to learn at home through computer, interactive video discs, and other technologies. (Be sure to indicate that these are only reasonable guesses, and stress the point that not everyone considers them desirable changes.)

5. Read and discuss part of John Naisbitt's *Megatrends*. (By close analysis of the work, help students identify some of the methods futurists use to predict the future—and note their limitations.)

6. Organize and hold a minidebate: Resolved, the American family will not change very much by the year 2010. (Teach a simplified debate format; note the limitations of debate as an inquiry process.)

7. Write a scene from a narrative about family life in the year 2010. (Teach students how to sketch in the setting, how to introduce and identify characters, how to refer incidentally to changes in the future without being too obvious about it.)

They then review their tentative list, to be sure that the experiences meet the criteria for quality learning and satisfy the requirements of the unit-planning guide. Their final step is to arrange the quality learning experiences into a useful sequence, again allowing the teacher some flexibility.

3. Review the quality learning experiences developed by the planning team. Check to be sure that they satisfy the requirements of the planning guide, that they meet the criteria of quality learning, and that they are arranged in a useful sequence. Make any changes suggested by this review.

7. Develop the unit and course tests.

By reviewing the course prospectus, the unit objectives, and the quality learning experiences, the developers should then rough out the unit and course examinations. Doing so will enable them to be specific about unit and course objectives: Whatever is tested is a key objective. The tests will also help teachers be clear about the measurable outcomes expected.

8. Package the product.

Put all the materials you have developed into a looseleaf notebook. The looseleaf format will make it easy for you to modify the course in the future. The format will also encourage teachers to add their own materials, for example, other resources, relevant professional articles, and teacher-developed lessons and learning materials. How much you include in the notebook will depend somewhat on teacher needs. The following items would probably be desirable.
1. A revised prospectus.
2. A summary of the knowledge base.
3. A list of all the units—title, general unit objective, probable length.
4. A revised set of quality learning experiences.
5. A list of the resources needed.
6. Copies of the unit and course examinations.

An Assessment of the Naturalistic Model

The naturalistic model described above has much to recommend it. Because it is sensitive to the political realities of curriculum making, it seems to result in products that have greater administrative acceptance. Because it reflects the way teachers actually plan, it is "teacher friendly"; they seem to like using the model. And it seems to result in more interesting and stimulating learning experiences, because it emphasizes the intrinsic quality of the experience. Its main drawback is its looseness. In the hands of the inexperienced and the careless, it can result in a seemingly random collection of entertaining activities that are not clearly related to the outcomes desired. Because of its looseness, it probably is more suited to disciplines (like English-language arts, social studies, and art) where tight articulation is not essential.

References

Clark, C. M. *Research on Teacher Planning: An Inventory of the Knowledge Base.* East Lansing, MI: Institute for Research on Teaching, Michigan State University, 1983.

Cohen, D. "Some Considerations in the Development, Implementation, and Evaluation of Curricula." *Technical Report 2.* Iowa City, IA: University Science Education Center, 1974.

Posner, G. J., and A. N. Rudnitsky. *Course Design: A Guide to Curriculum Development for Teachers.* 2d ed. New York: Longman, 1982.

Taba, H. *Curriculum Development Theory and Practice.* New York: Harcourt Brace and World, 1962.

Tyler, R. W. *Basic Principles of Curriculum and Instruction.* Chicago: University of Chicago Press, 1950.

Walker, D. F. "A Naturalistic Model for Curriculum Development." *School Review* 80 (1971): 51–65.

Wulf, K. M., and B. Schave. *Curriculum Design: A Handbook for Educators.* Glenview, IL: Scott Foresman, 1984.

7

How Do You Adapt the Curriculum to Respond to Individual Differences?

F or several decades now, educators have been attempting to "individualize" the curriculum or to provide "individualized" instruction. Their attempts have met with mixed success. Researchers now seem to believe that the term *individualized* is misleading and prefer to speak of *adaptive* curricular and instructional approaches. Definitions abound, but, in general, the terms *adaptive curricula* and *adaptive instruction* refer to processes of modifying what is taught and how it is taught in order to respond to the special needs of individual learners. Regardless of which term is used and how it is defined, interest in the topic continues. And there is now a growing body of research that can provide some guidance in making the curriculum more responsive to individual needs. This chapter will review that research briefly and then suggest some practical ways you can incorporate those findings in your own curriculum.

The Research on Adaptive Curriculums and Instruction

The following summary attempts to digest a complex body of research into some useful categories. However, because the topic is a complex one and the research continues to accumulate, be sure to stay current in this field especially.

These specific approaches seem to work.

Three specific approaches to adapting curriculum and instruction seem strongly supported by quality research.

1. MASTERY LEARNING. Mastery learning programs, although varying in specific attributes, share six features: clearly specified learning objectives; short, valid assessment procedures; preset mastery standards; a sequence of learning units; provision of feedback of learning progress to students; provision of additional time and help to correct specified errors (Anderson 1985). *Learning-for-mastery students have outperformed students in conventional classrooms on measures of achievement, retention, learning rates, attitudes, and self-esteem; the critical factors are setting appropriate standards (between 85 and 95 percent correct) and using effective feedback procedures* (Anderson 1985).

2. COOPERATIVE LEARNING. Cooperative learning models should have four key attributes: positive interdependence (achieved through mutual goals, divisions of labor, dividing resources or information among members, assigning students, giving joint rewards); face-to-face interaction among students; individual accountability for mastering the assigned materials; and appropriate use of interpersonal and small-group skills (Johnson and Johnson 1985). *Cooperative learning experiences, when compared with competitive and individualistic ones, result in higher achievement, promote greater competencies in critical thinking, develop more positive attitudes toward the subject, and lead students to believe that the grading system is fair* (Johnson and Johnson 1985).

3. COMPUTER-ASSISTED INSTRUCTION. Computer-assisted instruction (CAI) tends to take one of three forms: tutorial, in which the computer presents new information; drill and practice, in which the computer is used for remediation; and simulations, which involve the learner in

solving complex problems. *The average effect of computer-assisted instruction, when compared with traditional instruction, is to increase test scores from the 50th percentile to the 63rd percentile, with student attitude towards the subject being slightly more positive.* (Kulik 1983). Beyond this general finding, these specific findings might also be noted: Tutorial and drill modes are more effective for low-ability students than for middle or high groups; most of the studies showing a positive effect for CAI have used the computer as an adjunct, with the teacher readily available; foreign language and science are two areas in which CAI has been especially effective; and retention rates are somewhat lower with CAI than with conventional instruction (Forman 1982).

These specific approaches require additional research.

For four specific approaches to adaptation, additional research seems needed, because the evidence to this date seems somewhat inconclusive or negative in its implications.

1. ABILITY GROUPING. As noted in Chapter four, there are several types of ability-grouping plans often implemented as administrative means responding to individual differences by reducing heterogeneity. The research on ability grouping in general seems somewhat inconclusive. However, a rather careful and systematic analysis of all the quality research on ability grouping in the elementary schools concluded that there are some variations of grouping practices that seem differentially effective (Slavin 1986). *Within-class ability grouping in elementary mathematics seems effective; Joplin-plan and nongraded plans for reading instruction also seem to increase achievement.* (In the Joplin plan, pupils are assigned to heterogeneous classes for all areas except reading; during reading period, they are assigned to reading classes based on reading achievement.)

2. LEARNING-STYLES ADAPTATIONS. Many current programs are based on the theory that, because learning styles among students differ, the curriculum and the instructional practices should respond to those style differences. Some learning-style programs build on strengths: Identify the student's preferred style modalities and provide instruction that uses those strengths. (A good source for practical ways to match instruction with learning styles is Dunn and Dunn's 1975 book.) *The research evidence for adapting instruction solely on the basis of students' cognitive styles is not strong; there is only weak support for the recommendation that the instructional treatment should always be consistent with student learning styles* (Good and Stipek 1983). Some learning-style programs are based on diversity: In a

comprehensive set of learning experiences, be sure to provide some type of learning experience that uses each style preference. For example, McCarthy (1980) believes that teachers should provide for all learners an eight-step learning cycle that, according to her theory, both responds to strengths and remedies deficiencies. Although her system seems to embody sound theory, as yet it does not seem to be supported by any persuasive body of empirical evidence.

3. CONTENT OPTIONS. As explained earlier in this work, content-option "electives" attempt to adapt to individual abilities and interests by letting the students choose content emphases within a subject-matter area. Thus, instead of taking ninth grade social studies, students might choose from an array of nine-week electives like the following: Black American Heroes, Women in American History, The Hispanic Heritage, The City in History, and Utopian Communities in the United States. Although such content-option electives have been often indicted as contributing to the decline in college achievement and aptitude scores, there does not seem to be any quality research to support their use or discontinuance. As I have tried to show elsewhere (Glatthorn 1980) and as I indicate later on in this chapter, I believe that it is possible to design content-elective programs that will ensure mastery of essential skills while giving students some options. *Content options at the secondary level might be a useful approach to adaptive curriculums, if those options are carefully designed.*

4. SELF-PACED INSTRUCTION. Many programs attempting to adapt to individual needs have emphasized the use of self-paced instruction. In most of these programs, the curriculum is analyzed into several short components that are arranged in a controlled sequence; the learner is assessed and placed appropriately in that sequence. The learner works on self-instructional packets or lessons to achieve clearly specified objectives, working at his or her own pace and getting feedback about achievement. *Elementary and secondary students in self-paced instructional programs, when compared with those in conventional classrooms, did not gain more on achievement tests, did not gain more in critical thinking, and did not improve in self-esteem or in attitudes toward the subject* (Bangert, Kulik, and Kulik 1983). (Note that the research on self-paced instruction at the college level is much more positive in its findings.)

These combined approaches seem to show some promise.

Two approaches combine two or more elements in an attempt to derive multiple benefits. Both seem to show some promise.

1. ADAPTIVE LEARNING ENVIRONMENTS MODEL (Alem). According to its developers (Wang, Gennari, and Waxman 1985), ALEM combines direct instruction with aspects of open education. It begins with a diagnostic-prescriptive approach, in which students are assessed, are placed appropriately, work individually, and receive feedback about their performance. At that point students have some options: Those needing remediation receive it, and those achieving satisfactorily pursue enrichment activities. It also uses team teaching and emphasizes the importance of home involvement. *According to those involved with its development, ALEM can be implemented in a variety of school settings and does seem to facilitate student achievement; however, other researchers do not believe that its effectiveness has been soundly established.* (See, for example, Corno and Snow 1986.)

2. TEAM ASSISTED INDIVIDUALIZATION (TAI). Developed initially for elementary mathematics, TAI combines a type of individualized program with cooperative learning. Students are assigned to heterogeneous groups of four or five members. They are given a placement test and placed at the appropriate point in an individualized mathematics program, using a team-study method, in which students check each other's work and help each other improve. Each day the teacher works for 10 or 15 minutes with groups of students who are about at the same point in the curriculum. *The results of field tests indicate that TAI increases students' mathematics achievement more than traditional methods and suggest that students can take over most of the checking and routine maintenance functions of individualized programs (Slavin 1985).*

Using the Research to Develop School-Based Programs

How do you make use of this research in developing adaptive curricular and instructional models? I would first like to describe a general strategy that should be effective and then explain in somewhat greater detail two combined approaches that I think might have some promise.

1. Identify which schools will be encouraged to develop their own adaptive model. The argument here is for school-based decision-making—as opposed to district-based or department-based. Compelling all schools within a district to embrace a single model seems unwise. It ignores the importance of the school as the center for improvement efforts. It also ignores the finding that certain of these adaptive models are more effective at certain levels than others. It similarly seems unwise

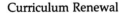
to permit too many different models to operate within one school. All the models require some complex modifications in the way curriculums are designed and implemented.

2. Determine which subject areas could best profit from adaptive modifications. Consider the nature of the subject itself. Some subjects, such as English-language arts and social studies, lend themselves more readily to the content-option approach. Other subjects, such as reading and mathematics, seem easier to adapt to computer-assisted instruction. Also review the data on student achievement, paying special attention to the less able and the gifted. In which subjects do those students seem to be achieving less than might be expected?

3. Next, meet with the teachers in those subject areas to review the research, to reflect about their area of the curriculum, and to make a tentative decision as to which adaptive approach seems most promising. It might be wise at this stage to encourage them to use either specific models strongly supported by the research or one of the combined models that seems promising. If they seem competent and creative, you may wish to encourage them as well to develop and test their own eclectic models or to test either of the models described below.

4. Provide extensive staff development to help teachers acquire the skills they need to develop and implement the model they have chosen. As part of that staff development, teachers should be involved in making the necessary curricular modifications and developing the needed student materials. It might be noted here that identifying the mastery and the team-planned enrichment curriculum, as recommended in earlier chapters, will facilitate such work.

5. Implement and test the adaptive model to be sure it is achieving its goals. Make any modifications indicated by the assessment.

6. If teachers are interested and have the time, encourage them to explore the other individualization models not yet strongly supported by the research. For example, some might wish to build into their mastery units some activities that make an explicit attempt to respond to learning style and modality differences. Because these other models are not strongly supported by the research, it might be wise to require extensive field testing before large-scale changes are made.

The "Cooperative Mastery" Model

The cooperative mastery model, which I have just begun to develop and test, combines the strongest features of mastery learning with the effective components of cooperative learning and uses the computer as an instructional adjunct. Admittedly eclectic and as yet not supported with summative research, it is an attempt to develop a practical model that would not require extensive restructuring of the school organization.

The first step in using the cooperative mastery model is to reconceptualize the existing curriculum. Instead of trying to cover the entire curriculum in the same way, a team of supervisors and teachers analyze the existing curriculum into three categories:

● Mastery concepts and skills that could best be taught with whole-class direct instruction techniques. In most instances about 50 to 70 percent of the existing curriculum might fall into this category.

● Mastery concepts and skills that could best be taught using cooperative learning processes. Approximately 20 to 30 percent of the existing curriculum might be in this category.

● Team-planned enrichment content that students could learn independently. About 10 to 20 percent of the curriculum might be in this category.

The mastery concepts and skills to be taught with a whole-class approach are developed into an appropriate number of mastery learning units, with a 90 percent standard established for mastery. The classroom teacher uses direct instruction techniques to teach each of these mastery units, probably taking about five to eight class sessions to teach the essential concepts and skills. At the conclusion of each unit, the teacher gives a unit test. Students who do not achieve at the specified 90 percent level spend additional time on remediation. Most use the computer for additional review and practice. Some are assisted by student tutors selected from the group that achieved mastery. While the nonachievers are getting corrective help, the rest of the achievers not involved in tutoring are working on the independent study units drawn from the team-planned enrichment curriculum.

When the remediation and independent study have been concluded, all students then work together in cooperative learning groups on the content previously identified for that purpose. In most instances, the cooperative groups would work collaboratively on laboratory and inquiry projects applying what has been learned in the mastery units and extending their knowledge.

The chief advantage of the cooperative mastery model is that it attempts to fit research-based approaches to the components of the curriculum where they might seem to work best. Rather than using direct instruction, or mastery learning, or cooperative learning with the entire curriculum, it attempts to find an optimal match. The chief drawback is that it requires a significant amount of curriculum development time to produce the materials needed to support the approach.

The "Quality Options" Model

The quality options model, also in the developmental stages, is an attempt to capture the strengths of the electives programs of the 1970s while avoiding their perceived weaknesses. The strengths were several. These short-term electives opened up the curriculum, enabling teachers to present greatly diversified offerings. They individualized by providing students with a choice of content, rather than having them all study the same curriculum. And they capitalized on teachers' interests and strengths, legitimizing teacher autonomy. Their weaknesses, however, were readily apparent. Too often, they turned the curriculum into a smorgasbord of unrelated offerings. And in too many instances the individual courses were too soft in an intellectual sense; they did not teach the essential skills and made few demands upon the students.

The quality options model essentially provides for a required one-semester course in which all essential content is taught, followed by two nine-week electives that provide for continuing emphasis of important process skills. Let me explain in general how they are designed, using an eighth grade social studies course as an example.

The first step in developing quality options is decide at what grade levels and in what subjects the quality options will be offered. In general I have been recommending to districts that the quality options be limited to grades 7 to 10, although this obviously is a matter of individual district choice. The rationale for limiting the options to these grades is that students in grades 5 and 6 are probably having enough problems handling the transition to departmentalized teams; and students in grades 11 and 12 probably need intensive and extensive preparation for college and career. I also recommend that the quality options not be offered in mathematics and foreign language, because the structure of those disciplines, as I perceive them, do not lend themselves to the options approach. However, each district needs to decide these matters for itself.

The next step is to take each existing one-year course (for the grade levels and subjects so identified) and reduce it to a required one-semester course. Supervisors and teachers should identify the essential concepts, information, and skills that all students should master—and that could

106

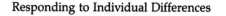

be mastered in one semester. You essentially ask the team this question: "What content is so important in this course that every student should know it, regardless of what electives he or she might take?" Obviously, this will require teachers to leave out some favorite content, but such a reduction is essential for the model to work.

For example, the eighth grade social studies team decided that their required semester course should provide students with a basic chronological framework for understanding United States history and should examine in some depth the critical periods of that history. Here are the essential units that the team decided to include in their required course:

1. The Founding of the Nation
2. The Civil War and Its Aftermath
3. The Industrial Age
4. United States as a World Power
5. The Continuing Struggle for Freedom

Next, identify the skills that should receive continuing emphasis in all elective courses, regardless of their content focus. These will most likely be process skills that can be applied to any content. Planning teams should be encouraged to identify a relatively small number of skills that can be systematically built into each "Quality Option" course. For example, the same team adapted a set of social studies skills recommended by one of the experts in the field (Crabtree 1983) in this manner:

BASIC STUDY SKILLS
1. Locate information in a variety of sources (including maps, charts, almanacs, newspapers, and journals).
2. Evaluate, interpret, and store information.
3. Categorize, organize, and retrieve information.
4. Communicate effectively in writing.

ANALYSIS AND DECISION-MAKING SKILLS
1. Define a problem.
2. Predict and hypothesize.
3. Differentiate between facts and inferences.
4. Compare through contrastive analysis.
5. Formulate inferences and conclusions.
6. Evaluate decision's consequences, make rational choice, and assess choice.

The next crucial step is to determine the organizing themes that will guide the development of the quality options. The organizing themes are governing principles that will connect and relate a series of electives. Their purpose is to bring some coherence into a set of offerings, avoiding the "patchwork quilt" effect of simply offering whatever courses teachers happen to like. For example, in English, an organizing theme might be "types of literature" or "ethnic perspectives on language and literature." The specific courses generated from the "types of literature" theme would carry titles like "Enjoying Poetry," "Discovering Drama," and "Reading Science Fiction."

The planning team determines which organizing themes will best meet these criteria: (1) themes are likely to respond to students' needs and interests; (2) themes appropriately reflect the structure of that discipline; and (3) themes will facilitate the inclusion of the continuing skills.

The eighth grade team chose two themes for their quality options—"introduction to the disciplines" and "discovering ethnicity." The first theme yielded this array of quality options: "An Anthropologist Looks at the U. S.," "A Sociologist Looks at the U. S.," "A Political Scientist Looks at the U. S.," "An Economist Looks at the U.S.," "A Psychologist Looks at the U. S." The second theme yielded this array: "Blacks in American History," "The Anglo-Saxon Heritage," "Eastern Europeans in America," and "The Hispanic Heritage." Thus, every student would be able to take one nine-week course that would present an introduction to the separate disciplines and one nine-week course that would emphasize a particular ethnic group.

Once the organizing themes have been identified, teachers collaboratively then develop the specific electives that will be offered in each nine-week cycle. Each team uses the planning processes described in the previous chapter to develop the quality options, using either the standard technological process or the naturalistic process. In either case it would be especially important to check to ensure that the continuing skills are taught and reinforced. The team planning the "Blacks in American History" course developed this set of two-week units:

Slavery as the Slaves Experienced It
Black Families in White America
Blacks and the Arts in the United States
Blacks as Political Leaders—Present and Future

They decided to emphasize the study skills in the first unit, providing students with sources that presented differing perspectives on the experience of slavery. They decided to emphasize analyzing and problem-solving skills in the last unit, helping the students make insightful analyses of a recent election and predictions about forthcoming elections.

References

Anderson, L. W. "A Retrospective and Prospective View of Bloom's *Learning for Mastery*." In *Adapting Instruction to Individual Differences*, edited by M. C. Wang and H. J. Walberg. Berkeley, CA: McCutchan, 1985.

Bangert, R. L., J. A. Kulik, and C. C. Kulik. "Individualized Systems of Instruction in Secondary Schools. *Review of Educational Research* 63 (Summer 1983): 143–158.

Corno, L., and R. E. Snow. "Adapting Teaching to Individual Differences Among Learners." In *Handbook of Research on Teaching* 3d ed., edited by M. C. Wittrock. New York: Macmillan, 1986.

Crabtree, C. "A Common Curriculum in the Social Studies." In *Individual Differences and the Common Curriculum*, edited by G. D. Fenstermacher and J. I. Goodlad. (Eighty-second yearbook of the National Society for the Study of Education.) Chicago: University of Chicago Press, 1983.

Dunn, R., and K. Dunn *Educator's Self-Teaching Guide to Individualizing Instructional Programs*. New York: Parker, 1975.

Forman, D. "Search of the Literature." *The Computing Teacher* 10 (1982): 37–51.

Glatthorn, A. A. *A Guide for Developing an English Curriculum for the Eighties*. Urbana, IL: National Council of Teachers of English, 1980.

Good, T. L., and D. J. Stipek. "Individual Differences in the Classroom: A Psychological Perspective." In *Individual Differences and the Common Curriculum*, edited by G. D. Fenstermacher and J. I. Goodlad. Chicago: University of Chicago Press, 1983.

Johnson, D. W., and R. T. Johnson. "Cooperative Learning and Adaptive Education." In *Adapting Instruction to Individual Differences*, edited by M. C. Wang and H. J. Walberg. Berkeley, CA: McCutchan, 1985.

Kulik, J. A. "Synthesis of Research on Computer-Based Instruction." *Educational Leadership* 41 (September 1983): 19–21.

McCarthy, B. *The 4MAT System: Teaching to Learning Styles with Right/Left Mode Techniques*. Barrington, IL: EXCEL, 1980.

Slavin, R. E. "Team-Assisted Individualization: A Cooperative Learning Solution for Adaptive Instruction in Mathematics." In *Adapting Differences*, edited by M. C. Wang and H. J. Walberg. Berkeley, CA: McCutchan, 1985.

Slavin, R. E. *Ability Grouping and Student Achievement in Elementary Schools: A Best Evidence Synthesis*. Baltimore: Center for Research on Elementary and Middle Schools, Johns Hopkins University, 1986.

Wang, M. C., P. Gennari, H. C. Waxman. "The adaptive learning environments model: Design, implementation, and effects." In *Adapting Instruction to Individual Differences*, edited by M. C. Wang and H. J. Walberg. Berkeley, CA: McCutchan, 1985.

Appendix. Recommended Sources for the Fields of Study

IN MOST INSTANCES THE MATERIALS LISTED BELOW HAVE BEEN RECOMMENDED by the professional associations indicated, who have also supplied the bibliographic information. In a few instances I have omitted items for the sake of brevity. Price information can be secured from the publisher.

Art

- From the National Art Education Association, 1916 Association Drive, Reston, VA 22091:
  - *Art Education: Elementary*
  - *Art Education: Middle/Junior High School*
  - *Art Education: Senior High School*
  - *Purposes, Principles, and Standards for School Art Programs*

- From the Getty Center for Education in the Arts, 1875 Century Park East, Suite 2300, Los Angeles, CA 90067:
  - *Beyond Creating: The Place for Art in America's Schools* (1985).

- From The College Board, Box 886, New York, NY 10101:
  - *Academic Preparation in the Arts: Teaching for Transition from High School to College* (1985).

Business

• From the National Business Education Association, 1914 Association Drive, Reston, VA 22091:

> Crews, J. W., and Z. S. Dickerson. *Curriculum Development in Education for Business* (1977 yearbook).
>
> Schimmel, W. T., ed. *New Directions in Teaching Business* (1984 yearbook).

English-Language Arts

• From the National Council of Teachers of English, 1111 Kenyon Road, Urbana, IL 61801:

> Copeland, E., ed. *Recommended English Language Arts Guides, K–12.*
>
> Glatthorn, A. A. *A Guide for Developing an English Curriculum for the Eighties.*
>
> Mandel, B. J., ed. *Three Language Arts Curriculum Models: Prekindergarten Through College.*
>
> NCTE Commission on Composition. *Teaching Composition: A Position Statement.*

• From the College Board, Box 886, New York, NY 10101:

> *Academic Preparation in English: Teaching for Transition from High School to College* (1985).

Foreign Language

• From the National Council on Foreign Language and International Studies, 45 John Street, New York 10038:

> Rosengren, F. H., M. C. Wiley, and D. S. Wiley. *Internationalizing Your School: A Resource Guide for Teachers, Administrators, Parents, and School Board Members*, 1983.

• From the American Council on the Teaching of Foreign Languages, Box 408, Hastings-on-Hudson, NY 10708:

> *ACTFL Provisional Proficiency Guidelines.*

• From the College Board, Box 886, New York, NY 10101:

> *Academic Preparation in Foreign Language: Teaching for Transition from High School to College.*

● From Phi Delta Kappa, Eighth and Union Sts., Bloomington, IN 47402:

> Benevento, J. *Issues and Innovations in Foreign Language Instruction*, 1985.

Health

● From the National Center for Health Education, 30 E. 29th Street, New York, NY 10016:
> *How Healthy is Your School?*
> *Growing Healthy: A Program for Children Grades K–7.*

Home Economics

● From the Bennett & McNight Publishing Company, Peoria, IL 61615 (Recommended by the American Home Economics Association, 2010 Massachusetts Avenue NW, Washington, DC 20036):
> Laster, J. F, and Dohner, eds. (1986). *Vocational Home Economics Curriculum: State of the Field.*

Mathematics

● From the National Council of Teachers of Mathematics, 1906 Association Drive, Reston, VA 22091:
> *Agenda for Action: Recommendations for School Mathematics of the 1980s.*
> *Computers in Mathematics Education.*
> *Mathematics for the Middle Grades.*
> *The Secondary School Mathematics Curriculum.*

● From the College Board, Box 886, New York, NY 10101:
> *Academic Preparation in Mathematics: Teaching for Transition from High School to College*, 1985.

Music

● From the Music Educators National Conference, 1902 Association Drive, Reston VA 22091:
> *The School Music Program: Description and Standards* 2d ed., 1986.

Reading

● From the International Reading Association, 800 Barkdale Road, Box 8139, Newark, DE 19714:
  Duffy, G. J., ed. *Reading in the Middle School*, 1974.
  Graham, K. G., and H. A. Robinson. (1984). *Study Skills Handbook: A Guide for All Teachers*.
  Harker, W. J., ed. *Classroom Strategies for Secondary Reading* 2d ed., 1985.

Science

● From the National Science Teachers Association, 1742 Connecticut Avenue NW, Washington, DC 20009:
  An NSTA Position Statement: Science Education for the 1980s.
  Holdzkom, D., and P. B. Lutz. *Research Within Reach: Science Education.*

● From the College Board, Box 886, New York, NY 10101:
  Academic Preparation in Science: Teaching for Transition from High School to College, 1985.

Social Studies

● From the National Council for the Social Studies, 3501 Newark Street NW, Washington, DC 20016:
  In Search of a Scope and Sequence for Social Studies. 1983.
  Downey, M. T., ed. *History in the Schools*, 1985.
  Stanley, W. B., ed. *Review of Research in Social Studies 1976–1983*, 1985.

● From the College Board, Box 886, New York, NY 10I01:
  Academic Preparation in Social Studies: Teaching for Transition from High School to College, 1985.

● From the Association for Supervision and Curriculum Development, 125 North West Street, Alexandria, VA 22314:
  Morrissett, I., ed. *Social Studies in the 1980s: A Report of Project SPAN.*

Technology

● From the International Technology Education Association, 1914 Association Drive, Reston, VA 22091:

> *Technology Education: A Perspective on Implementation*, 1985.
> Boben, D. K. *Guidelines for Equity Issues in Technology Education*, 1985.
> Gettle, K. E., and D. Maley, eds. *Selected Questions Pertaining to Teaching Technology Education*, 1984.
> *The Professional Improvement Plan: Delivering Services to the Technology Educator.*